HOME HANDYMAN

HOME IMPROVEMENTS AND EXTENSIONS

AURA BOOKS

CONTENTS

Editor: Mary Lambert
Designer: Eljay Crompton

This edition published by
Aura Book Distribution Limited
2 Derby Road
Greenford, Middlesex

Produced by
Marshall Cavendish Books Limited
58 Old Compton Street
London W1V 5PA

© Marshall Cavendish Limited 1984
ISBN 0 86307 260 7
Printed and bound in Milan, Italy by New Interlitho

Home Improvements and Extensions
shows you how to repair and improve your
home with the minimum of fuss and
bother. All the information you need is
here—from choosing a tool kit to carrying
out basic home repairs. There's a range of
exciting projects plus advice on how to
extend your home into the roof space or
out into the garden

A basic DIY kit

A good selection of tools is a pleasure to own and an investment for the future. Anyone who takes pride in doing a good job will enjoy working with the best tools and in the majority of cases these will never need replacing as long as they are properly treated and maintained.

Holding and supporting

One of the most useful and important tools in carpentry is a workbench. Having somewhere to do your joinery without having to clear the kitchen table makes life much easier, and if you have a proper bench you can store your tools in it tidily and conveniently.

A solid and secure vice—either built-in, or of the clamp-on type—is indispensable for securing timber and other items on which you are working, and G-cramps will help to secure longer lengths of work in addition to their normal duties.

Measuring tools

Accuracy in measuring and cutting is reflected in the quality of your finished work so you should always buy the best and most robust measuring instruments available in your price range.

Buy a good quality—and preferably a long—spirit level for checking levels and verticals. If you can afford it choose one with an adjustable glass which you can use for checking angles as well. A less accurate, but nonetheless useful, tool is a simple plumb bob and line which can be used for checking verticals on a larger scale. A steel rule is also an essential item.

A woodworkers' try square is essential for checking right-angles as well as the accuracy of planed timber edges—look for one with a sprung steel blade and a stock protected by a thin brass strip. You will also need a combination square for marking angles and mitres: this has a stock which slides along a calibrated steel blade that is used as a depth gauge. A marking gauge is essential for scribing marked-up joints and for multiple marking-up on a large job.

Cutting tools

Accurate cutting is an essential requirement of almost every DIY job so a variety of reliable cutting tools is essential. Two saws—a panel saw which should be about 550mm long and a tenon saw which should be about 250mm to 300mm long—are enough, though separate rip and cross-cut saws are better than a general-purpose panel saw.

Carpenters' chisels are almost indispensable, but they must be looked after properly if they are to give the best results. A selection of three or four bevel-edged chisels is the best choice for a basic tool kit—6mm, 12mm, 25mm and 37mm blades are the most widely used. Whether your chisels have wooden or plastic handles you should never use anything except rawhide, plastic or wooden mallets to hit them with.

Bench planes are available in a wide variety of types and sizes, but an excellent basic choice is a unit about 250mm in length and about 50mm in width. A handyman's knife is a useful item with its interchangeable and replaceable blades.

Abrasives

Files and rasps for shaping and smoothing metals and timber are a necessary part of any tool kit, but because they are fairly expensive you should buy them only when you need them. From the wide variety of shapes and styles available a half-round file is probably the best choice as it can be used for both flat work and concave work such as smoothing the insides of holes.

1 Cramps are vital in most types of carpentry work. G-cramps are useful in securing longer pieces of timber in addition to their normal purpose. Sash cramps are good for long pieces of timber but are expensive. Less expensive, and equally good, are cramp heads pictured in the illustration

2 Accuracy in measurement in any type of do-it-yourself is essential if you are going to achieve the perfect finish. Therefore buy the best try and combination squares and marking and sliding bevel gauges. Also don't forget the importance of having a long, good quality spirit level and the useful bob and line

3 If you find you need to do a great deal of joinery work, a mortise gauge saves a lot of time. It is a necessary item for accurately marking out mortise and tenon joints. A sharp, handymans' knife with changeable blades is also very useful. It is particularly good for marking cutting lines

4 One of the most important items you can buy for your tool kit is a good quality steel rule. They come in lengths from 150mm to 1m and apart from being ideal for the usual measuring tasks, they can also be used as straightedges and cutting guides. A folding boxwood rule for general joinery work is also handy

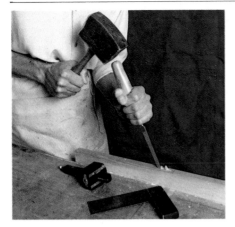

5 Chisels are indispensable tools for joinery work and need to be carefully looked after. To have a selection of about three or four bevel-edged chisels is the ideal number. Always use rawhide, plastic or wooden mallets to hit your chisels or you may seriously damage the handles over a period of time

6 Planes are again very useful items for the do-it-yourselfer. Bench planes are the best ones to handle the rougher planing work, but block planes complement these very well. They can be used for those finer, more meticulous, aspects of cabinet work, such as bevelling or trimming or just to plane end grain

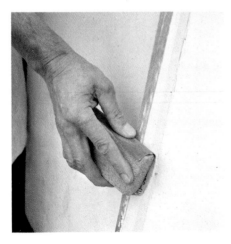

7 Sanding requires a firm touch and you must at all times use the correct grade of paper for the relevant task. Glasspaper is best for most timber finishing while wet and dry paper is better suited to metal and glass fibre work. Harder masonry or painted surfaces may call for something harder, like silicon carbide

8 A power drill is one of the most useful assets of your tool kit as it is so versatile both inside and outside the house. Buy the best drill you can afford. Multi-speed units which have a full range of accessories and a hammer action for drilling through masonry are a particularly good choice

9 A comprehensive screwdriver kit, which includes some cross-head screwdrivers and both long and stubby flathead examples, does not cost a great deal of money and can be used almost anywhere. The kit is essential to all those fiddly everyday tasks. Use a good file to keep the screwdrivers true

10 If you embark on a major home improvements project, you will need some specialized tools to work with. A 2kg club hammer and steel bolster are the first items needed for breaking up masonry and stripping old plaster. They can also prove extremely good for prising up nailed-down old floorboards

11 Pliers are other tools which always come in handy—self-locking pliers, such as a Mole wrench, are particularly good when dealing with nuts, bolts and compression joints in pipework. A comprehensive set of spanners is also very good to have as is a tin of penetrating or possibly lubricating oil

12 Tools which are used for cutting obviously require the most frequent attention—chisels and planes particularly need regular sharpening. To ensure a good cutting edge, a honing guide and an oilstone are worthwhile investments. Saws and drill bits should be taken to an expert to sharpen

A good selection of abrasive paper together with a rubber or timber sanding block is essential both for finishing timber and for preparing surfaces for painting and papering.

Drilling

The most useful and versatile drilling tool that you can buy is of course a power drill. It is worth spending a little extra on a unit made by one of the more reputable manufacturers for which a full range of accessories is available. You can buy these as the need arises, but it is worth buying a multi-speed drill at the outset so that you can use all accessories properly on both metal and masonry.

Despite this, a hand-operated wheel brace is essential for times when there is no power or where an electric drill would be too powerful.

Another essential item for use especially with metal is a countersink or rose bit—these are available for both hand drills and ratchet braces.

To mark the hole before drilling use a bradawl for timber, and a centre punch for metal.

Hammers and screwdrivers

The choice of tools under this heading is vast, and you can spend a great deal of money buying tools that you rarely, if ever, use. For general work you can get by with three hammers: a claw hammer of around 680g is a good all-purpose tool, while a 225g cross-pein hammer is best for driving in panel pins and small nails. An engineers' or ball-pein hammer is the best for metalwork and for driving masonry nails.

For joinery work and chiselling you will need a carpenters' or joiners' mallet.

Other tools

As well as the tools mentioned above, you will find some others extremely useful. Chief among these is a pair of pliers: the most common types are the bull-nosed variety, but needle-nosed pliers are also extremely handy for electrical work.

Build a mitre jig

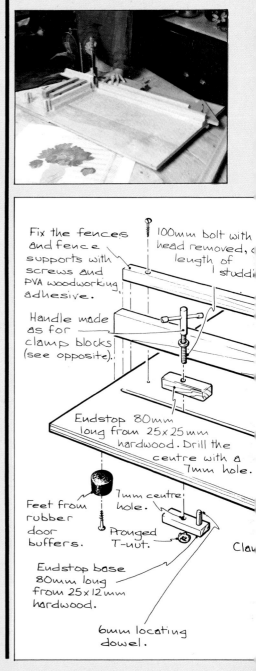

Fix the fences and fence supports with screws and PVA woodworking adhesive.

100mm bolt with head removed, length of studdi

Handle made as for clamp blocks (see opposite).

Endstop 80mm long from 25 x 25 mm hardwood. Drill the centre with a 7mm hole.

Feet from rubber door buffers.

7mm centre hole.

Pronged T-nut.

Endstop base 80mm long from 25 x 12 mm hardwood.

6mm locating dowel.

Cla

This mitring jig is good for all kinds of projects, but is ideal for picture frames using frame mouldings.

It has two fences so that the parts are aligned squarely, and two sets of saw guides for square and angled cuts. There are two clamps to hold the workpiece in position and an adjustable end stop for gauging the length of the sections.

It is not very complicated, except for the clamps, but the accuracy of assembly will determine the accuracy of the jig.

Start by cutting out the baseboard and marking two square lines on it for the fences. Mark the cutting lines at the right angles to this. Then cut the slot for the end stop. Glue and screw the fences in—make sure you get them dead square, otherwise the jig will be inaccurate.

Make up the saw guides from dowel and tubing. Drill the baseboard and press them into position. Do not fix so they can be replaced. Make sure they are set on the cutting lines.

Make up two clamps from hardwood blocks. The clamping mechanism is made from nuts and bolts and tubing. Drill the blocks for fixing screws. When using, adjust the clamps to lock timber, butt it against the end stop and cut between the saw guides making sure that you do not cut into the wood of the jig itself.

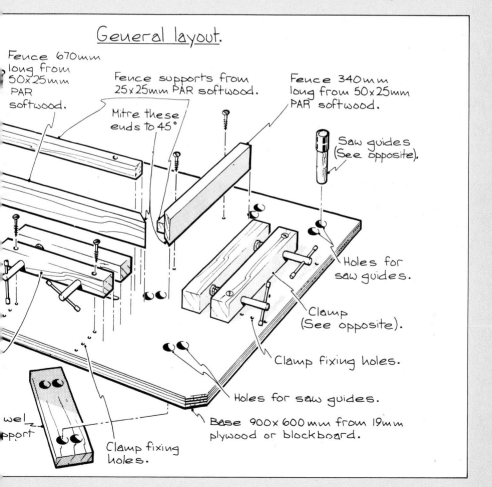

General layout.

Fence 670mm long from 50x25mm PAR softwood.

Fence supports from 25x25mm PAR softwood.

Mitre these ends to 45°

Fence 340mm long from 50x25mm PAR softwood.

Saw guides (See opposite).

Holes for saw guides.

Clamp (See opposite).

Clamp fixing holes.

Holes for saw guides.

Base 900x600mm from 19mm plywood or blockboard.

Dowel support

Clamp fixing holes.

Using a chisel

Knowing how to use a chisel correctly is one of the most important aspects of carpentry. And once you have mastered the skills and techniques involved, a whole new range of do-it-yourself projects becomes possible.

Types of chisel

The chisel is the basic wood-shaping tool and is used for paring, cutting joints and chopping out areas of wood for hinges and other fittings.

Bevel-edged chisels have tapered edges which allow the chisel to get easily into tight corners. They are ideal for cutting dovetails and shallow housings, such as hinge recesses, and for vertical paring.

Firmer chisels have strong blades of rectangular cross-section which make them stronger than bevel-edged chisels and thus more suitable for heavy work such as fencing, frame construction and notching out for pipes running over joists.

Mortise chisels are the strongest chisels of all and are designed to withstand both

A. Three types of chisel. (a) Bevel-edged chisel has a blade with tapered sides, to get right into the corners.
(b) Paring chisel has a long bevelled or rectangular blade. (c) Firmer chisel, with its strong rectangular blade, is used for heavy work

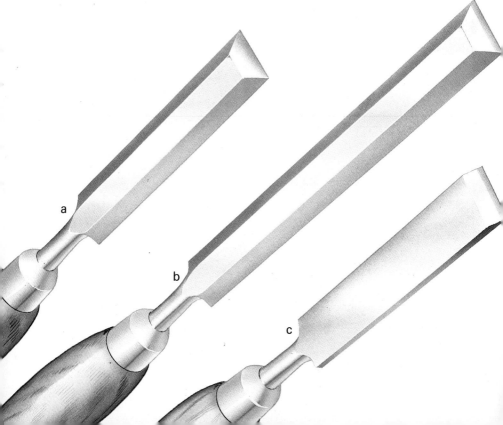

a

b

c

continual striking with a mallet and the levering action required when cutting the mortises for mortise-and-tenon joints.

Paring chisels have long blades of either firmer or bevel-edged type. The long blade is so designed for reaching into awkward corners and for paring out long housings, such as those used in bookcases.

Buying chisels

Bevel-edged and firmer chisels are available in a wide range of widths from 1mm to 38mm. Initially, a set of 6mm, 12mm and 25mm chisels should be adequate for most requirements. Mortise chisels do not come in such a range of sizes and it is unlikely that anything other than 6mm, 8mm and 12mm mortises will ever be required. Buy paring chisels only when the need for a particular one arises.

Chisel safety

Chisels are often supplied with plastic guards which fit over the end of the blade. If the chisels you choose do not come supplied with guards, it is well worth buying a set.

Horizontal paring

Horizontal paring is a technique used when constructing joints—such as housing joints for supporting the ends of shelves and halving joints used in framework.

When making such a joint, define the area of the slot by marking out width lines on top of the wood, and width and depth lines on both sides. Make a saw cut slightly to the waste side of each width line and cut down to the depth line.

Hold the wood securely in the vice so that it will not move as you work and make sure that it is horizontal (fig. 1). Hold the chisel in both hands, safely behind the cutting edge, with the elbow resting comfortably on the bench. This gives extra control over the chisel's movement.

Start by chiselling out the waste adjacent to the sawn lines, making angled cuts to half way across the wood (fig. 2). Push the chisel firmly, holding it at a slight angle, keeping your arm horizontal and level with the work. When the cuts are half way across the joint, reverse the wood in the vice and complete the angled cuts from the other side (fig. 3).

Now turn the chisel over so that the bevel is facing downwards and remove the bulk of the remaining waste by slapping the handle of the chisel with the palm of your hand (fig. 4). Because the bevel side is facing down, the chisel blade works its way up to the surface and no levering action is needed to clear the waste. Again chisel only half way across the joint, then turn the wood around and work from the other side with the bevel side of the chisel facing upwards once more (fig. 5).

When most of the waste has been removed, work the chisel across the joint, keeping it absolutely flat across the bottom, to shave off the last fibres of wood (fig. 6). Finally, hold the chisel vertically in one hand and work the blade into the corners to clean them out and sever any remaining fibres (fig. 7).

Vertical paring

Vertical paring is necessary when you wish to round off a corner or to make a curve in a piece of wood.

Hold the wood on a bench hook, to protect the surface of the work bench, and support the other end, if necessary, with a timber offcut of the same height as the hook (fig. 8). Hold the chisel upright in both hands with the thumb of the upper hand over the top of the handle to give control and downward force.

Mark the required curve on the wood and cut off the corner, to an angle of about 45°, with a tenon saw. Holding the chisel as described, pare off the corners left by the saw cut. Keep paring off the corners, taking off thin slivers of wood not more than 1mm thick (fig. 9). If you take off thicker cuts than this, the extra effort involved may cause you to lose control of the chisel.

1 For horizontal paring, hold the wood firmly and securely in the vice so that it does not move as you chisel. Rest your elbow comfortably on the bench

2 Hold the chisel with both hands, keeping them behind the cutting edge and pare angled cuts which are adjacent to the sawn guidelines

5 Turn the wood in the vice once again, and remove the remainder of the waste from the other side. The bevel edge should then be facing up once more

6 When most of the waste has been cleared out, work the chisel across the joint with its blade flat against the wood to remove the fine shavings

9 Remove slivers of wood, gripping the blade tightly between your fingers. Hold your thumb over the handle to provide more downward force

10 When cutting a mortise, cramp the wood and carefully protect it with a timber offcut. The tail of the cramp should then be beneath the work

3 When the angled cuts are half way across the wood, turn it around in the vice and then finish the cuts from the other side

4 Turn the chisel over so that its bevel-edged side is facing down and quickly slap the handle with the palm of your hand to remove the waste

7 To sever any remaining fibres in the corners, work the blade carefully into each corner with the chisel held strongly in one hand

8 For vertical paring, place the wood on a bench hook and support the end with a timber offcut. Keep your head bent closely over the work

11 Keep your body right behind, and completely in line with, the work and drive the chisel firmly into the wood with a wooden mallet

12 For paring out long housings, use a paring chisel. The long blade can be worked flat over a long distance to achieve an even finish

11

13 To sharpen the blade of a chisel, hold it at an angle of about 30° on to an oilstone. Rub the blade slowly in a figure of eight motion

14 When a wire edge begins to form, turn the blade over. Rub the other side over the oilstone keeping the blade flat upon the surface

Work as closely in to the curve line as possible, then finish off by smoothing with a file.

Cutting a mortise

A mortise is a rectangular slot cut into a piece of wood into which a tongue—called a tenon—from another piece of wood is fixed. The mortise and tenon make a strong joint which is used to form T-shapes in frames. The mortise should always be made with a mortise chisel.

To mark out a mortise accurately you need a mortise gauge. Using a chisel of the exact width of the planned mortise, set the gauge to the chisel blade and mark out the width lines on the wood. With a try square as a guide, draw the two setting-out lines which determine the length of the mortise.

When cutting a mortise, the wood should be held securely on a solid part of the bench rather than cramped in the vice: as the chisel is struck with a mallet, it would dislodge the wood from a vice. Use a G-cramp to hold the wood in position and protect the top with a timber offcut (fig. 10). Make sure that the tail of the cramp is beneath the work or injury may result. Drive the chisel into the wood with a mallet.

Start by driving the chisel into the

mortise to dislodge a deep wedge of waste. Use three separate strokes of the chisel to remove the wedge, making it equal on both sides. Keep your body behind, and in line with, the work (fig. 11). Work, with a series of small chops, from the centre towards one of the setting-out lines keeping the chisel in the same vertical plane at all times. Stop at the line, turn the chisel round and approach the other setting-out line with a further series of chops.

Clear out the waste and dislodge another wedge in the centre to the depth of the finished mortise. A band of tape wrapped around the chisel blade to the required depth makes a good depth indicator. Chop up to both setting-out lines, again to the required depth.

Sharpening chisels

No matter how correct your technique or how expensive your chisels, you cannot produce good work with a blunt chisel. You should always check that cutting edges are sharp before use and hone them if necessary.

Sharpen a chisel on an oilstone. Apply a light oil liberally to the surface to prevent metal filings clogging the stone. Hold the chisel with one hand gripping the handle, the other steadying the blade.

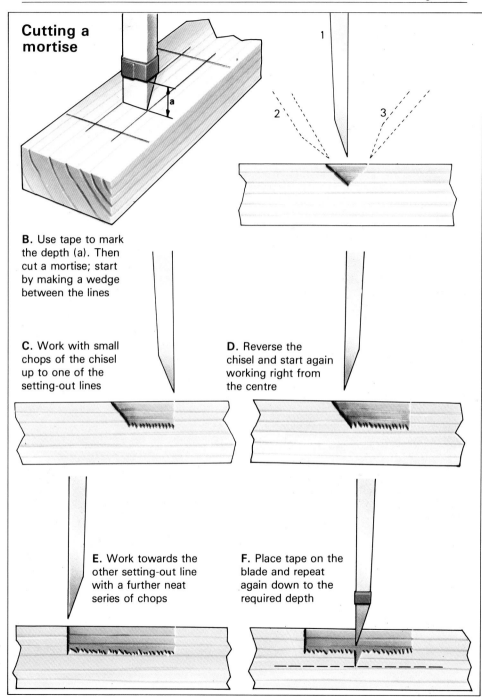

Cutting a mortise

B. Use tape to mark the depth (a). Then cut a mortise; start by making a wedge between the lines

C. Work with small chops of the chisel up to one of the setting-out lines

D. Reverse the chisel and start again working right from the centre

E. Work towards the other setting-out line with a further neat series of chops

F. Place tape on the blade and repeat again down to the required depth

Fixing wood to wood

Nails and screws are the two most important fastening devices used in carpentry, but how well they do their job depends almost entirely on how correctly they are used.

Tools

The two hammers used most frequently in carpentry are the claw hammer and the cross-pein, or 'Warrington'. The first is useful for levering out old nails and lifting floorboards while the second is more suited to finer nailing work.

If you are starting a tool kit, opt for a 450g claw hammer and a 280g Warrington. Later, you can add a 100g 'pin' Warrington for light, accurate nailing and pinning.

For burying nails below the surface of the wood, you need a set of nail punches. These come in quite a variety of sizes—to suit different sizes of nail—and help to avoid bruising the wood with the hammer head.

Some kind of drill is essential for screwing work. A power drill is the obvious choice because of its versatility, but where there are no power points or access is limited, a wheel brace (hand drill) will serve well.

To drill larger holes by hand, you need a swing brace and a set of special bits—not a priority for the beginner's basic tool kit.

Good quality screwdrivers are essential to any tool kit and cabinet screwdrivers, with blades of about 300mm, are the most useful. Two of them—one with an 8mm tip and one with a 6.5mm tip—should cover you for most jobs. To deal with crosshead, Philips or Posidriv screws, you need screwdrivers with the appropriate tips.

Using a hammer

Using a hammer properly requires a little bit of practice. Take a firm grip right at the end of the handle and form your arm into a right-angle, looking straight down on the work as you do so. Start the nail by tapping it lightly, keeping your wrist controlled but flexible and letting the

Above: Start short nails with a cross-pein hammer. Tap gently with the wedge end until they stand firm, then drive in firmly with the hammer face

Above: Very small nails and pins should be held with a pair of pliers. Use the cross-pein hammer to hit the nail with fairly gentle taps

hammer head do the work.

On well-finished work, remember not to drive nails right in—leave a bit protruding for the hammer and nail punch to finish off.

Start light nails or tacks with the cross-pein by tapping gently with the wedge end of the hammer head. Drive them home with the hammer face using a number of fairly gentle taps rather than

Commonly used nails

Round wire

For rough carpentry work: large ugly head ensures a firm grip. Liable to split wood

Oval wire

Commonly used in carpentry. Oval cross section makes it unlikely to split wood if the long axis follows the grain

Lost head

General carpentry nail. Head can be punched below the surface and the hole filled

Panel pin

Small nail for securing light pieces of wood; usually used in conjunction with glue

Clout nail

Large headed for fixing roofing felt, sash cords, wire fencing to wood. Galvanized for outdoor work

Flooring brad

Used to hold down floorboards. Good holding power and unlikely to split wood

Glazing brad

Headless: used to hold glass to picture frames and lino to floorboards. Will not grip if driven too far in

Masonry nail

Hardened steel nail for fixing wood to soft brick, breeze block and concrete

Hardboard pin

Special head shape countersinks itself in hardboard and can be filled over

Upholstery nail

Decorative head used to cover tacks in upholstery work

trying to knock them in with one blow, which will probably bend the nail.

Nailing techniques

For accurate, well-finished work, nails alone do not normally make a strong joint. However, if the nails are angled in opposition to each other, a reasonable joint can be made. When used in conjunction with one of the modern woodworking adhesives, a very strong joint can be achieved. Seldom are nails driven straight—a stronger joint can be made if they go in at an angle or *skew*.

Removing nails

The claw hammer is used to remove partially driven nails. To avoid damaging the surface of the wood, place a small offcut under the hammer head before you start levering. Extract nails with a number of pulls rather than trying to do the job in one.

Use pincers to remove small nails and pins which are difficult to grip with the claw hammer.

Drilling screw holes

All screws must have pilot holes made before they can be driven home. For screws into softwood smaller than No. 6 gauge, make these with a bradawl. Drive it into the wood with its chisel point across the grain, to avoid splitting.

Screws into hardwood and screws into softwood larger than No. 6 gauge need

Nailing tips

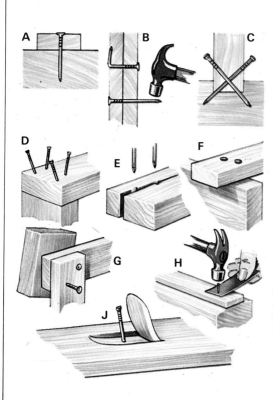

A. Use nails about 3 times as long as the workpiece. Always nail smaller to larger. B. On rough work, clench-nailed joints are much stronger. C. Skew-nailing is one of the best ways of securing a housing joint. D. When nailing into end grain, drive in nails at opposing angles. E. Driving more than one nail along the same grain line risks splitting the wood. F. Nail small battens overlength to avoid splitting the end. Afterwards, saw or plane off the excess. G. Avoid 'bouncing' by placing a block under the workpiece. H. Small nails can be positioned with the aid of a cardboard holder.
J. Secret nailing. Prise up a sliver of timber with a chisel. Glue down after nailing

two pilot holes. One is for the thread—the pilot hole—and one for the shank—the shank hole.

For all except the largest pilot holes, use twist drill bits. Those for pilot holes should be the same size as the screw core to which the threads are attached. Those for the shanks should match them.

Screws: types and uses

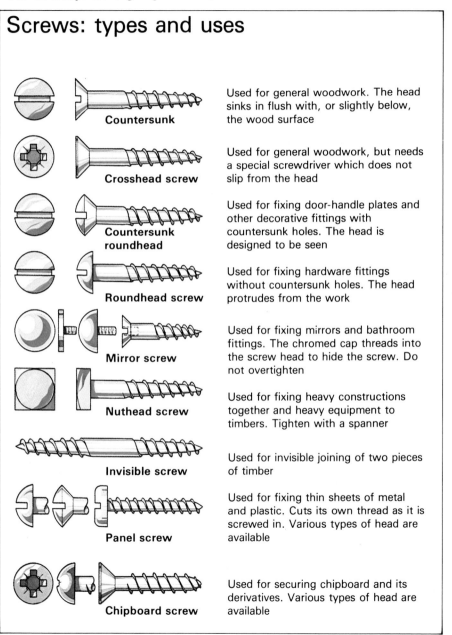

Countersunk

Used for general woodwork. The head sinks in flush with, or slightly below, the wood surface

Crosshead screw

Used for general woodwork, but needs a special screwdriver which does not slip from the head

Countersunk roundhead

Used for fixing door-handle plates and other decorative fittings with countersunk holes. The head is designed to be seen

Roundhead screw

Used for fixing hardware fittings without countersunk holes. The head protrudes from the work

Mirror screw

Used for fixing mirrors and bathroom fittings. The chromed cap threads into the screw head to hide the screw. Do not overtighten

Nuthead screw

Used for fixing heavy constructions together and heavy equipment to timbers. Tighten with a spanner

Invisible screw

Used for invisible joining of two pieces of timber

Panel screw

Used for fixing thin sheets of metal and plastic. Cuts its own thread as it is screwed in. Various types of head are available

Chipboard screw

Used for securing chipboard and its derivatives. Various types of head are available

When drilling pilot holes, mark the required depth on the drill bit with a piece of masking tape. This will tell you when to stop and cannot damage the workpiece should you overdrill.

As with nailing, where two pieces of wood are to be fixed together, screw the smaller to the larger. Drill the shank hole right through the smaller piece so it is pulled down tight as the screw is driven home. If the shank hole goes only part of the way through you will find it very hard to pull the top piece of wood down tight and may risk breaking or damaging the screw. Brute force should never be used—it indicates that either the thread hole or the shank hole is too small.

Countersinking

Countersinking is normally the easiest way of recessing screw heads flush with, or below, the surface of the wood. The recess is made with a countersink bit after the pilot has been drilled, to the same depth as the countersunk screw head. Take particular care if you are countersinking with a power drill or the recess may accidentally become too large.

Drilling techniques

Using the correct drilling technique makes all the difference to the quality of the finished work. Whether your drill is power or hand operated, you should always hold it at right-angles to the work surface so that the pilot hole is straight. If you find this difficult, rest a try square upright near the bit and use it as a guide.

With bit drills, operate the drill in bursts and lift it frequently to allow debris to escape. To give yourself as much control as possible, always hold the drill with both hands and never press too hard—you are bound to overdrill.

Keep the chuck key taped to the cable, so it is handy whenever you want to change bits.

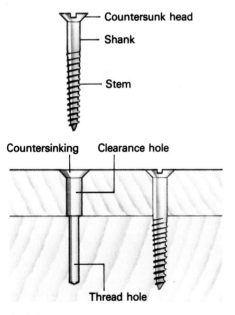

A. Drill two pilot holes for each screw — the top one to accept the shank in a 'push fit', the bottom one should be about two sizes smaller

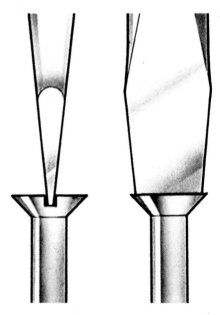

B. See that the screwdriver blade fits the screw head exactly and that the tip is kept ground square. If not, you run the risk of 'chewing up' the screw

Using a hand-operated wheel brace requires slightly more effort, but gives more control than a power drill. When drilling vertically, grip the handle with your thumb on top. Turn the wheel steadily to avoid knocking the drill out of line.

To drill horizontally, grip the handle with your thumb towards the wheel. Alternatively, where a side handle is fitted, grasp this in one hand while you turn the wheel steadily with the other.

Driving screws

Always make sure that the tip of your screwdriver is in good condition and that it fits exactly into the slot in the screw head. A blade which is too narrow or rounded damages the slot, while too wide a blade damages the wood.

When using a pump-action screwdriver, hold it firmly in both hands—one on the handle, the other on the knurled collar just above the bit—and make sure that you are not off-balance. Any loss of control could cause the blade to slip out of its screw slot and damage your wood.

To make screwdriving easier, the screws can be lubricated with wax or candle grease before driving. Brass screws are quite soft, and to prevent damage when screwing into hardwood, the resistance can be lowered by driving in a steel screw first.

Below: When you have acquired some of the basic carpentry skills you could easily progress to doing something more ambitious, like making this attractive bunk bed for children

The art of planing

A plane's job is to slice off unwanted portions of wood, reducing the wood to the exact size required and leaving it smooth and flat.

Bench planes

These are made up of the same parts and have the same adjusting and sharpening procedures. They come in four lengths. The jointer plane is the longest, measuring approximately 550mm, the fore plane is about 450mm, the jack plane is 350–375mm and the smooth plane 200–250mm.

The plane blade has two angles forming the cutting edge—the ground angle of 25° and the honed angle of 30°. The plane's ground angle is already formed on a new plane and will need only occasional renewing on a grinding stone, but the honed angle has to be sharpened before you can use the plane.

Taking apart and sharpening

Referring to the diagram detailed, remove the lever cap by releasing the cam and sliding the cap upwards until it will lift off. Remove the plane blade and the cap iron. Place them on a flat surface and undo the cap iron screw. Slide the blade forward, twist it through 90° and remove from the cap iron.

If you have a honing guide for sharpening the blade, set this up according to the manufacturer's instructions. Alternatively, use an oilstone box with a medium stone.

Use enough oil to keep the surface of the stone moist. Hold the plane iron so the blade is at 90° to the stone with the bevel side of the blade down on the stone. Tilt the iron until you feel the bevel flat on the stone—this will be about a 25° angle. Tilt through another 5° to get a 30° angle. Then rub the blade evenly up and down the stone, maintaining the angle.

Above: A fairly long plane should be used for long pieces of wood so that the plane levels out the timber rather than following any profile it might have. The plane should be held comfortably with the body weight positioned over the top of it to give all the pressure that is needed to make the cut

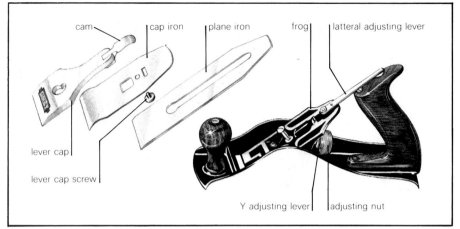

cam   cap iron   plane iron   frog   latteral adjusting lever

lever cap

lever cap screw

Y adjusting lever   adjusting nut

Above: A new plane is easily taken apart for sharpening the blade

Continue doing this until you feel a burr or wire (a roughness) on the flat side of the blade. When you feel it burred evenly all the way across, turn the blade over and place it flat on the stone. Holding it flat with both hands, move it up and down at a slight angle until the burr has been removed from the edge.

Repeat on a fine stone and then, if you want a very sharp edge, do the same again on a leather strop impregnated with motor car valve grinding paste to provide a good abrasive.

Re-assembling

To put the plane together again, hold the cap iron screw side up and place the blade at right-angles to it over the screw. Slide the blade so that the screw goes three-quarters of the way up the slot, then twist it back through 90° and slide it back until only 1.5mm of blade projects beyond the cap iron.

Finger-tighten the screw and readjust the blade to a clearance of 0.5–0.7mm. Hold the blade flat on a bench and tighten the screw. Place the blade back on the plane—taking care not to damage the sharpened edge—so that it lies flat on the frog. Then replace the lever cap. Look along the bottom of the plane from the

front at eye level and move the lateral adjusting lever to the right or left, if the blade is not level. It must be exactly level to give an even cut.

Block planes

These are very like the bench planes but they are smaller. They are made up of similar parts but there are fewer of them. They have to be taken apart and the blade sharpened in exactly the same way as the bench plane.

The standard type has the same cutting angle as a bench plane. Others have a cutting edge of 20° and 12°, which make it easier to use on small items. They can be used one-handed quite easily.

Block planes are particularly suitable for using on small pieces of timber, for working on the end grain of timber and for trimming plastic laminates.

Preparation

Put the wood on a solid, level surface so that it will not move while you are planing. Have the end of the wood against a stop.

If you are supporting the workpiece in a vice, make sure that it is sandwiched between two offcuts to prevent the jaws from bruising the wood.

The frog part is adjustable, which means that the mouth of the plane can be altered according to the type of material

1 Always remember to make sure before you even contemplate a planing job that your plane is very sharp. Otherwise it will badly tear the surface of the wood, probably making it unusable. Moisten the stone with oil. Tilt the iron to a 30° angle and then rub the blade evenly up and down the stone maintaining that particular angle

2 Keep rubbing the blade evenly up and down until you feel what is known as a burr or wire—basically a roughness—on the flat side of the blade. When you can feel it has got an even roughness, turn the blade over, putting it flat on the stone. Then holding it flat move it up and down at a slight angle to remove the burr from the edge

5 Then hold the blade completely flat on a bench or workmate and firmly tighten up the screw with a large screwdriver. Place the blade very carefully back on the plane—making sure that you do not damage the sharpened edge—so that it lies completely flat on the frog section. Then you can safely replace the lever cap

6 Then look along the bottom of the plane from the front angle, and at eye level, and move the lateral adjusting lever to either the right or left so that the blade is level and protrudes less than 0.5mm. This adjustment is particularly critical as the blade must be completely level to give the necessary even cut when you are using the plane

3 If you want a very sharp edge on your plane, rub it at a slight angle on an oiled leather strop to provide a good abrasive. Put the plane back together again by holding the cap iron, screw side up, and place the blade at a 90° angle to the screw. Slide the blade so the screw moves further up the slot and then twist it back through 90°

4 Slide the screw further back until only about 1.5mm of blade is still visible projecting beyond the cap iron. The next thing to do is finger tighten the screw and to accurately readjust the blade to a clearance of 0.5–0.7mm. You can probably judge with your eye, but if not, measure the clearance just to be on the safe side

7 Now the plane is sharpened and ready to use. Put the wood on a solid, level surface or have it fixed in a vice between wood offcuts so that the jaws do not damage your piece of wood. Hold the plane with both hands and with your body balanced over the top, push the plane over the wood, keeping the cuts shallow but very even

8 When you are planing long square edges, you will need to apply more pressure on the front knob of the plane at the beginning of each stroke. So use your fingers to support the plane and help keep it in a square position. At the end of the stroke, apply pressure to the back of the plane. Always make the stroke along the whole length of wood you are planing. For rough planing and soft timbers, the blade should be set with half to three-quarters of the mouth open. For fine finishing of hard woods and for planing end grain, the frog should be adjusted to give a very fine mouth opening of about 1.5mm.

Method

Hold the plane firmly but comfortably with both hands and with your body balanced over the top of the plane. Push the plane forward over the wood keeping the cuts shallow and even. Never plane against the grain of the wood or the blade will catch on the ends of the fibres.

If you are planing correctly you should be producing ribbon-like shavings of equal width and thickness.

When planing long edges apply more pressure on the front knob of the plane at the beginning of the stroke, even out the pressure in the middle of the stroke and at the end of the stroke apply more pressure at the back of the plane. Make the stroke the whole length of the wood each time.

As you plane, make sure by frequent checking with the try square that the edge you are working on is at right angles to the other surfaces. And use the edge of the try square, or a steel rule, to see that the edge is straight.

End grain

If you are planing end grain, cut the wood 6mm longer than it needs to be. Put the piece of wood upright in a bench vice, with a waste piece of wood behind. Plane across both pieces of wood—that way any splitting will occur on the waste wood rather than the wood you want to use.

Alternatively, you can bevel all the four corners and then plane from one end towards the middle. Turn the wood around and plane from the other end towards the middle. Remove the piece left in the middle very carefully. Even when using a method such as this, take great care to avoid putting undue pressure on the plane.

9 If you are planing correctly you should be producing long ribbon-like shavings of equal thickness and width. Do not spoil the rhythm of planing by stopping in mid-stroke. When you are planing across a wide width of wood, twist the plane so that it is at an angle to help reduce the natural resistance of the wood

10 To plane end grain, put the wood securely in a vice with an offcut fitted neatly behind it and then plane smoothly across both pieces. Another method is to bevel all four corners of the wood and then plane evenly from one end to the middle. Turn over the wood and repeat the process

Repairing window sills

The purpose of a window sill is to protect the wall underneath the window from rain. Although this may not seem necessary—after all, the rest of the wall is not protected in this way—rainwater striking the glass panes forms a concentrated, downward-running cascade which could penetrate a masonry wall

Above: Obvious signs of rot, if left unattended, can cheapen the appearance of your entire property

or even start rot in wooden siding.

Some typical sills are illustrated. They project well beyond the frame of the window itself so that rainwater is

25

directed well clear of the supporting wall.

Unless rainwater runs off quickly, wooden sills may rot and stone or cement sills crack through frost action.

A drip groove on the underside of the sill is a small but important feature. Whatever the angle of slope on the top surface, some rain inevitably creeps around the front face of the sill; accumulated drips then work along the bottom edge and onwards to the wall—where they can attack the joint with the sill. The drip groove prevents this by halting the water's progress, causing it to form into larger droplets that then fall harmlessly to the ground.

Some sills are formed in one piece with the rest of the window frame. Others are installed separately and if any joint between the two is left unprotected or badly sealed, you can almost certainly expect trouble later on.

Dealing with design faults

If you want to avoid recurring problems, it is important to correct any design faults during the course of routine maintenance or repair work.

Start by checking the drip groove. Appearance can be deceptive: there may be a drip groove, but well hidden under layers of paint. Probe around to see if you can find one and, if you do, scrape the recess completely clear then prime and paint it, taking care not to repeat the fault.

Where there is no groove, you might be able to rout or chisel one. But a stop of some form is a much easier solution which should work just as well. You can make the stop from a length of quadrant (or even square) beading and fix it to the underside of the sill with impact adhesive, about 35mm back from the front edge.

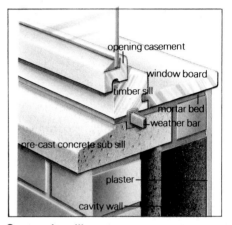

Composite sill

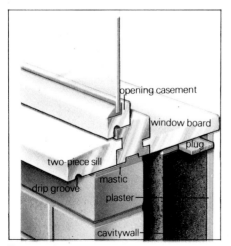

Tongued-and-grooved sill

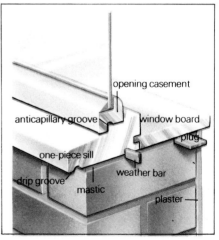

Projecting sill

Prod a wood sill with a pointed blade or bradawl to check for wet rot, and look for fine cracks and flaking on stone or concrete sills—typical signs of an inadequate slope.

A wooden sill is easily corrected by planing it to a suitable slope, though you can do this only if the timber is sound and deep enough.

A stone sill can be repaired and sloped by forming a mortar fillet on top.

Paint the surface with PVA adhesive so that the new mortar mix of one part cement to three of sand adheres properly. Run over this with an offcut of timber to give the slope you want, then remove the former and shape a rounded front edge.

Rotten window sills

If you have caught the rot in good time you may need to do nothing more than burn off all the paint on the sill, scrape the surface back to sound timber, and flood the area with wood preservative before repainting.

But if the damage is at all extensive, it is sensible to cut out the affected part and replace it. Some joinery stockists sell ready-shaped sills and if you can find one which has the same profile as your sill (or nearly so), it can be used for patching gaps. Otherwise you have to trim a piece of suitable timber to the correct shape.

Most modern wooden sills are made of softwood—usually redwood—which is perfectly suitable providing it has been properly treated with pressure-impregnated preservative.

Hardwood is a better material for sills because of its resistance to decay, but there are problems. Susceptibility to surface 'checking' may make traditional materials difficult to paint, while some hardwoods such as Ramin have poor resistance to decay.

Replacing a sill

If the sill is formed in one piece with the window frame, you must cut it free at a suitable point in order to replace the whole sill. If possible, arrange the cut so that the joint with the new sill will be covered by the next window frame member up. Otherwise simply cut off a generous width of sill, well beyond the depth of rot.

Clean up the cut face of the remaining part of the sill by chiselling and planing until it is smooth and flat. Treat the face generously with preservative (fig. 4).

The new sill is bonded firmly to this surface. Although galvanized screws driven in at angles from below through the two pieces might do in some cases, a better solution is to make dowel joints between the two.

Whatever main method of fixing you choose the two surfaces must also be glued together, using a urea or resorcinol formaldehyde adhesive. When the wood is well bonded, rake out all the gaps between the new sill and the wall or the old sill and flood them with preservative. Finally, pack the gaps with a suitable waterproof mastic.

To repair just a small section of sill, cut out the affected part with a saw and chisel then use this as a template to cut the patching timber to size. Thoroughly treat the new wood with preservative, then glue it in place with a urea or resorcinol formaldehyde adhesive. Finally, screw the patch to the existing sill using galvanized screws countersunk well below the surface. Cover the heads with filler.

Painting

Prevention is much better than cure, so making sure that your window sills are properly painted is essential.

The old paint will probably have to be removed completely if it is in poor condition and in this case burning off is better than using stripper because it keeps the wood dry. Sand the surface smooth afterwards and treat any knots with knotting compound to seal them. Rub a fine wood filler into the surface to seal the grain—do not forget the ends of the sill. Finally paint with primer, undercoat and two top coats, making sure that no bare timber is left overnight.

1 Use a pointed tool and knife to investigate the extent of the rot in the window sill. You should expect trouble at exposed joins in old sills. Then, carefully mark an angled cut line on each side and well clear of the rot, and use a tenon saw to completely remove the rotten section

2 Chisel well into the sound wood to the rear, levelling the wood as you proceed, so that the replacement pieces will fit easily into the gap. Then from direct measurements, cut the necessary replacement sill sections. Carve or rout a drip groove to join the one already in existence

5 Another task before fixing this sill section is to apply a suitable adhesive—urea resorcinol formaldehyde adhesive is best—to all the contact areas on the sill and the new piece of wood. The adhesive used should always be a waterproof type

6 Now carefully place the wood section into position and immediately drill holes with a power drill for the secondary fixing. Do not forget to countersink the holes so they will not be visible. Then firmly fix the plated screws in with a screwdriver

3 Where the sill rot has spread to nearby framework, a replacement section must be fitted. Build this up from any suitable pieces of timber you might have around. It is sometimes easier to shape wood in situ. Use countersunk fixing screws, and then plane the wood to reduce it to the correct size

4 Before you permanently fix the first sill piece in position, one of the things you must make sure you do is to apply liberal quantities of a good wood preservative with a paintbrush to all the points of contact. Make sure you work the preservative well into all the cracks and crevices

7 Check the remaining pieces of wood that need to be fitted for accuracy of measurement and then coat these and the contact positions with the waterproof glue. Then screw into position as the previous section and make good any gaps with a well-known make of filler

8 The last thing to complete the repair is to plane all the new sill pieces so that they blend in completely with the existing section of sill. Then carefully sand down the new wood and filled sections ready for the necessary priming and subsequent painting

Door repairs

Above: This small kitchen is made even more cramped by a door which opens inwards. By rehanging the door to open outwards more space is immediately created

There is nothing more annoying than a door which is difficult to open and close. And although the trouble can usually be put right quite easily, neglecting such a door may cause more extensive damage which is costly and difficult to repair at a later date.

Choosing hinges

Plastic, nylon, or—better still—pressed steel hinges are suitable for light internal doors, but if you are fitting hinges to a heavy, outside door, use the strong type made of cast steel.

By finding out the thickness, weight and height of your door, you can estimate what size of hinge you require. For example, a lightweight door, 32mm thick, would need a 75mm × 25mm hinge, whereas a heavier door, 45mm thick, might require a 100mm × 38mm hinge. To find the size of a hinge, first measure its length and then the width of one of its leaves to the middle of the knuckle where it swivels.

Most doors are fitted with butt hinges and you can buy either the fixed or the rising variety. The rising butt hinge allows the door to rise as it is opened but shut down closely on to a carpet or threshold as it closes. This means that though the door does not scrape against floor coverings, it will stop draughts.

Marking and fitting

Before you fit the hinge decide which side you want the door to open. Panelled doors can be hinged on either edge but most modern flush doors can only be fitted with hinges on one edge.

Once you have decided which edge of the door is to be hinged, arrange it so that it is resting on the opposite edge. Support the door by wedging it into a corner, cramping it to the leg of a table, or by holding it in a vice.

The best positions for the hinges are 215mm from the top of the door and 225mm from the bottom, but make sure that this does not leave them over any joints or the door may be weakened.

Use a marking knife and try square to mark the hinge positions on the door edge, starting from the knuckle edge where the hinge will swivel. Mark across all but 6mm of the edge then continue on to the face of the door, marking the thickness of one hinge leaf (fig. 1).

Next, open one of the hinges and lay it in position on the door edge to check that the lines you have drawn are accurate. Hold the hinge in position and use a marking knife to mark each end (fig. 2). Then neatly scribe the width and depth of a hinge leaf on to the door edge and frame (fig. 3).

Cutting out

The hinge recesses are now ready to be cut out. Use a bevel-edged chisel and start by chopping downwards across the grain in a series of cuts 5–6mm apart. Leave a thin uncut border of about 2–3mm around the three edges. Now hold the chisel flat, bevel side up and pare away the chipped-up timber. Finally, keep the flat side of the chisel parallel to the door edge and clean out the rest of the recess (fig. 4).

The hinge should now press firmly into place flush with the surrounding timber.

Fixing hinges

Once the hinge is comfortably in position, carefully mark the screw holes with a sharp pencil then remove the hinge and remark the screw centres with a centre punch. Try to mark these a little off centre—towards inside of the recess— so that once the screws are inserted, the hinge will be pulled snugly into position.

Drill pilot holes to the depth of the screws and then clearance holes deep enough for the screw shanks. For heavy butt hinges use No. 7 or No. 8 × 38mm screws. Insert the screws so that they finish level with, or slightly below, the hinge plate (fig. 5).

Fitting the door

Position the door in its frame by supporting the base with wooden wedges made from offcuts (fig. 6).

With all types of hinge, make an allowance at the base of the door for any proposed floor covering and adjust the gap as necessary by altering the positions of the wedges. Then scribe around the hinges with a marking knife to mark their positions on the door frame.

With the door removed from the frame, mark out the hinge recesses—their length, width and depth—accurately with a marking knife and adjustable try square. Use the same technique to cut the recesses as you used for those on the door.

Replace the door and position it exactly using the wooden wedges, then

1 Before fixing new hinges, stand the door on its edge and support it securely with a vice firmly clamped to either the top or bottom. Accurately position the hinges 215mm from the top of the door and 225mm from the base. Remember to keep the hinges well clear of any joints on the door

2 You should then use a sharp marking knife and a try square to indicate the position of the hinges on the door edge, starting from the knuckle edge where the hinge will actually swivel. Make marks across all but 6mm of the edge and then carry these marks right on to the face of the door

5 Mark the screw holes slightly off centre towards the inside of the recesses. This allows the hinge to bed securely once it is fixed. Drill the pilot and clearance holes and then insert the screws, with a big screwdriver, so that they are slightly below the level of the hinge plates

6 Actually positioning the door into the frame is not that easy a task. So to make it easier for yourself, fit wooden wedges, made from any spare offcuts, under the base of the door. This then gives you the flexibility you need to lift or lower the door and adjust it to exactly fit the frame as is required

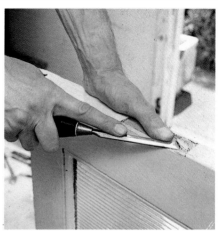

3 Then set a marking gauge to the width of a hinge leaf and scribe this on the door edge between the two other lines previously marked. Then reset your marking gauge to the depth of one hinge leaf and mark this on to the face of the door frame right in between the two knife cuts

4 Use a bevel-edged chisel to cut out the hinge recesses. Make a number of cuts about 5–6mm apart so that you leave an uncut border around the edge. Cut out the chipped-out timber in the hinge recesses with a chisel — held bevel side up — until the recess has become completely clean and smooth

7 Broken or damaged joints can be strengthened by first drilling out the old wedges to a depth of 75mm using a 15mm twist power drill. The holes can than be filled with 15mm thick dowels which have been glued. These should be chamfered at one end and have longitudinal cuts

8 When removing a planted door stop, first use a blunt, wide chisel and a mallet to actually prise the stop away from the door frame. The next stage is to insert the claws of a hammer well into the gap. The door stop can then be slowly worked loose and away from the nails holding it to the frame

9 When rehanging a door which was hinged on the other side, pin pieces of wood block to fill all the gaps and then plane the door smooth

10 If the door is rehinged to swing in a different direction, a new door stop must be added to the door frame so that the door will close properly

tap the hinge leaves into place in the waiting recesses. Finally, mark and predrill each screw hole then insert one screw in each hinge so that you can check that the door opens and closes properly.

Sticking doors
If a door sticks and you can find nothing wrong with the hinges, it may be that part of the door frame has swollen. Where the swelling is slight and there is plenty of clearance between door and frame, investigate the possibility of bringing the swollen part away from the frame by either packing or deepening one of the hinge recesses.

Where the swelling is more severe, you have no choice but to plane off the excess and redecorate the door. The planing can be done with the door in situ providing you first wedge the base, to take the weight off the hinges.

Older doors and those particularly exposed to damp may warp or become loose at the joints, causing them to fit badly in their frames. In the case of slight warping, one answer is to make a small adjustment to one of the hinge positions

so that you take up the twist. Do this on the frame—not on the door.

However, a more satisfactory solution is to remove the door so that you can cramp and strengthen the frame. Take off all the door furniture—the hinges, knob, lock, key escutcheon—place it flat on a workbench, then cramp the frame square using a sash cramp with a long bar.

Where gaps appear in the joints, scrape out any dust, accumulated grime and old glue with a chisel or knife. Then bring the joints together by cramping across the frame in two or more places. Use softwood offcuts to protect the door from being bruised by the cramps.

Next, drill out the old wedges holding the tenons at each frame joint to a depth of 75mm; use a 15mm twist drill bit. Make up some 85mm lengths of 15mm dowel with longitudinal cuts in them to allow for compressing (fig. 7) and chamfers at one end to give a snug fit.

Liberally smear each piece of dowel with external grade waterproof woodworking adhesive then drive them home into the drill holes with a mallet. Check that the cramps are still holding the frame square by measuring across the diagonals—which should be equal—and leave the adhesive to set. When it is dry, cut off the excess dowel with a tenon saw and finish the edges in the normal way.

Changing direction

It is often useful to change the direction in which a door swings—to make more space in a small room for example—or to hang it from the opposite side of the frame.

Making a door open in the opposite direction involves removing and resiting the door stop, altering the hinge rebates and possibly changing the door furniture. You may or may not have to change the hinges, depending on what type you have. Ordinary butt hinges can simply be used the other way up.

Removing a planted stop: Remove the door from the frame and clear the space around you. Then use a blunt, wide chisel and mallet to cut into the joint between stop and frame and lever the stop away. The stop is bound to be securely fixed and you may have to use considerable force. The job becomes easier when you can insert the claws of a claw hammer and ease the stop away, working upwards from the base of the door (fig. 8).

Once the door stop has given way, remove any old glue or chipped wood with a chisel, plane and glasspaper.

Removing a rebated stop: Start by measuring by how much the stop protrudes then mark this amount down and around the outside face of the frame with a marking gauge.

Next, take a tenon saw and make a series of cuts 12–18mm apart in the top corners of the door frame. Remove the waste between these with a wide chisel as you would that in a halving joint. This done, you can insert a rip saw or power saw and cut downwards through the remainder of the door stop. Afterwards, plane the cut timber flush with the rest of the frame and use a chisel to clean up the corners.

Rehanging

When you come to rehang the door, the hinge recesses may well have to be moved. Do this by chiselling them across to the other side of the frame. Then make up wood blocks to fill the now unused parts of the recesses and pin and glue these in place (fig. 9).

Refit the door stops—or make up new planted ones in the case of rebated stops —in accordance with the new door position. Make sure that the stops are firmly pinned and glued (fig. 10).

If the door lock or latch is handed, you must exchange it for a new one and fit it according to the manufacturer's instructions. Alter the position of the striker plate and make good the old recess as you did the hinge recesses. Finally, rehang the door as described above; start by fitting the hinges.

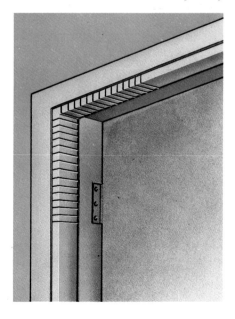

A. Left: If you want to remove a planted stop, first make a series of cuts 12–18mm apart around the corners of the stop on each side of the door. Chop away the waste wood with a mallet and chisel. Then insert a rip saw or power saw and cut away the stop across the top and down both sides of the door

Basic plastering repairs

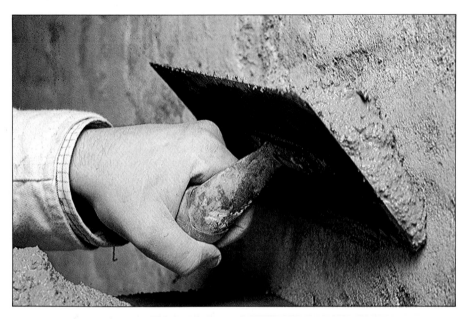

Plaster can be applied to solid surfaces, such as bare brick, cement rendered brick, building blocks or concrete, and to surfaces to which a key for the plaster—such as metal lathing or wooden slats—is attached. On most solid surfaces two coats of plaster, known as the floating coat or undercoat and the setting or finishing coat, are applied. When lathing is fixed to the surface, an additional first rendering coat is necessary called a pricking up coat.

Plasters

The main constituent of ready-mixed plasters is gypsum, calcium sulphate, which has been partly or wholly dried in a kiln. The extent to which the gypsum has been dried, and the addition of

Above: Plaster is applied to a wall with a laying-on trowel. When you are spreading plaster, keep the trowel's top edge tilted towards you

further constituents during manufacture, determine the type and grade of the plaster.

Lightweight, pre-mixed gypsum plasters are the most commonly used nowadays, by both professionals and amateurs. They come in several types, each used for a specific purpose.

Browning is a floating coat (undercoat) plaster used on semi-porous surfaces such as bricks, clinker blocks (breeze blocks) and concrete blocks.

Bonding is a floating coat plaster used on less porous surfaces such as poured concrete, where getting good adhesion is difficult.

Finish plaster is used for the thin surface coat that is applied over the undercoat.

Special plasters are also available for stopping and skimming plasterboard.

If in doubt on which undercoat plaster to use, ask the advice of your builders' merchant.

Always store plaster in a dry place. If any water comes into contact with plaster before it is used, the properties of the plaster will be altered. You should use plaster as soon as possible' after buying, as the retarder—the constituent which governs the setting time—grows less effective with time. Plaster is usually date stamped on the bag and, whenever possible, you should use the plaster within six weeks of the date.

Tools for plastering

Most of the tools you need for plastering can be made yourself. They include:

Spot board: This can be a piece of exterior-grade ply about 1m² and is used for holding the mixed plaster. A couple of coats of exterior-grade polyurethane wood lacquer will help to preserve the wood. The board should be placed on a stand—a wooden crate or sturdy stool will do—at a convenient height from the floor. The board should overhang the stand slightly so that the hawk can be held under the edge when transferring the plaster on to it.

Hawk: A board about 300mm × 300mm for carrying plaster from the spot board to the work area and for holding the plaster as you work. Professionals use aluminium hawks with moulded-on handles, but you can get by quite comfortably with a home-made one. Cut your square from an offcut of timber or plywood and screw on a handle about 200mm long cut from 50mm × 50mm timber with the edges rounded off.

Laying-on trowel: Used for applying and spreading the plaster. It has a rectangular steel blade about 280mm × 120mm attached to a wooden handle. Some trowels have curved handles which are easier to grip. A trowel of good quality is important as it is hard to obtain a smooth finish with a worn or inferior blade.

Gauging trowel: Available in a variety of sizes and used for repairing areas too small to be worked with the laying-on trowel. Also useful for mixing plaster.

Below: Tools for plastering include (**A**) home-made scratcher, (**B**) laying-on trowel, (**C**) gauging trowel, (**D**) hawk, and (**E**) skimming float

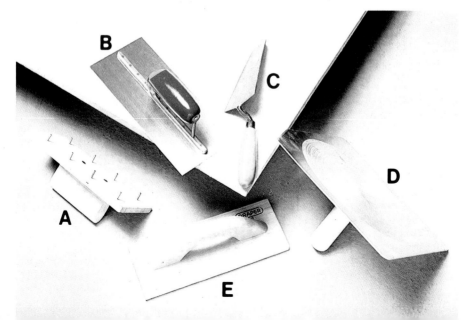

1 Before you begin to plaster a large patch on the wall, use a good hammer and a bolster to cut straight lines round the area. This will help to make the subsequent plastering that much easier to apply and level

2 Scrape some of the mixed plaster from the spot board on to the hawk with the laying-on trowel. Then make sure you carefully trim off any excess plaster. Hold the trowel at an angle over the hawk and take up a small amount of plaster

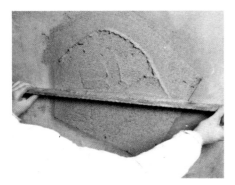

5 Now take a straight-edged length of wood that is a little longer than the patch and draw it upwards in even strokes so that you make sure the plaster is completely flush with all the edges of the patch

6 Next, again use the laying-on trowel to finally trim any excess amounts of plaster. These may have accumulated around the edges of the patch and possibly on to the surrounding area of the main wall

Skimming float: Used for levelling the floating coat. Plastic skimming floats, light in weight and non-warping, are available. But you can make a serviceable float from a smooth, flat, straight-grained piece of wood about 280mm × 120mm × 10mm, with a wooden handle.
Scratcher: To ensure the adhesion of the next coat of plaster, the surface of an undercoat is scratched over. A suitable

scratcher can be made by driving a few nails into a piece of wood and then cutting off their heads with a pair of pincers or pliers.

In addition, you will need two buckets —one for mixing the plaster in and one for holding water—a distemper brush and straight-edged rules of various lengths depending on the size and nature of the job. Also required, for chipping off

3 The next step is to hold the trowel against the wall surface, keeping its upper edge tilted backwards at an angle of about 30°. Then smoothly draw it upwards, spreading the plaster evenly over the patch

4 Keep applying further amounts of plaster from the trowel until the patch is completely filled in. The new plaster should then be smooth and level with the surface of the old surrounding plasterwork

7 To make room for the necessary, final coat of plaster, you will need to go over the surface of the undercoat again with the skimming float. This will help to really flatten the plaster and cut it back

8 Using the straightedge again, draw it across the patch once more to check that the undercoat surface is level all over and that it is actually slightly lower than the old plaster on the wall which surrounds it

old plaster, are a hammer and a bolster.

Preparing the surface

Before you start, clear the room of furnishings as much as possible, as the plaster dust will fly everywhere and can scratch polished surfaces. Cover what you cannot remove with old dust sheets. Have ready a suitable receptacle to receive the old plaster.

If the wall behind the plaster is of new brickwork it will need only brushing down and damping with clean water before you start to apply the new plaster.

Concrete wall surfaces require special preparation as their smoothness provides a poor 'key' for plaster and their density gives low suction. Before you plaster, paint the concrete with a PVA adhesive such as Unibond, applied neat.

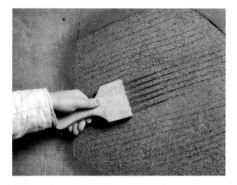

9 Run the scratcher lightly across the undercoat surface to form thick and noticeable ridges. This helps to key the surface of the patch, ensuring that the coat of finishing plaster does adhere properly. Then mix up the necessary finishing plaster and apply it smoothly and accurately to the patch using the laying-on trowel. Use firm pressure all the time and make quick, upward movements with the trowel

10 As the finishing plaster begins to set, dampen it slightly with the distemper brush. However, take great care not to use too much water at this point or it will become too messy. Wet the laying-on trowel and smooth it over the surface in slow, circular movements. Finish off with light, upward strokes and you will begin to see how well the new plaster does blend in with the old surface of the wall

Mixing the floating coat

When mixing plaster of any type use only water that is fit for drinking. Any impurities in water may be detrimental to the properties of plaster.

Pre-mixed lightweight undercoat for plastering small areas should be mixed a third of a bucket at a time. This is sufficient to cover a patch of about 300mm × 300mm to a depth of about 10mm. If the area to be plastered is larger than this, it is better to mix further amounts later. Pour water into the bucket first, then add the plaster. If the plaster is put in first, it clogs when the water is added and sticks to the bottom of the bucket. Add the plaster, while stirring the mixture with a stick, until a stiff but workable mix is obtained.

Whenever you have finished mixing any plaster, pour it on to the spot board. Then clean the bucket out immediately, or any remaining traces of plaster will set and then be extremely difficult to chip off. Traces of old plaster in the bucket will also speed up the setting time.

Applying the floating coat

Mix the floating coat plaster and place it on the spot board. Hold the hawk beneath the overhang of the spot board—if you are right-handed hold the hawk in your left hand and vice versa. Use the laying-on trowel to scrape some plaster on to the hawk them trim away any excess (fig. 2). Tilt the hawk and 'snatch up' a small amount of plaster on to the trowel. Keep the trowel horizontal until the edge connects with the wall, then tilt the outer edge upwards until it is at an angle of about 30° to the wall (fig. 3).

Begin in the centre of the patch and work upwards, exerting slight pressure. Keep the laying-on trowel at an angle, with its upper edge clear of the wall, so that plaster is fed to the wall all the time (fig. 4).

If the patch is 10mm deep or less, fill it until the new plaster is level with the old surrounding plaster. If the patch is more than 10mm deep, do not attempt to fill it in with one coat as this results in the plaster shrinking back from the edges and cracking. Instead, fill the area to half its depth, then use the scratcher to key the plaster with criss-cross lines. Apply a second layer of plaster when the first layer is dry.

Now, take a straight-edged rule a little longer than the patch and, working from the bottom upwards, draw the rule from side to side over the plaster to make it flush with the edges (fig. 5). Fill in any hollows with more plaster and draw the rule over the surface again.

To make room for the finishing coat, the plaster in the floating coat must now be cut back to a depth of 2mm lower than the surrounding plaster. First, flatten and cut back the floating coat with the skimming float (fig. 7). Next, run the scratcher over the surface of the floating coat to provide a key for the finishing coat (fig. 9). Then, go over the plaster with the skimming float again to flatten the burrs left by the scratcher. The scratch marks should remain but their edges should not protrude too far.

Below: If a patch of plaster has to extend round a corner, nail a thin piece of batten to one side of the corner and plaster up to it

Clean the surrounding wall area to remove any adhering plaster and leave the floating coat to set. Ready-mixed plasters take between 1½ and 3 hours to set.

Before mixing your finishing coat, clean all tools and the spot board.

Mixing the finishing coat
Lightweight finishing plasters are applied thinly so they can always be mixed in a bucket. Pour water into the bucket until it is about a quarter full. Slowly pour in the plaster until it appears above the water and stir with a stick. Once the plaster has settled, add more and keep stirring until the paste reaches the consistency of thick cream. Then pour it on to the spot board.

Applying the finishing coat
Lightweight finishing coat plaster dries very quickly. So until you are experienced, mix and apply only enough to cover a small area at a time. Scrape some plaster from the spot board to the hawk and lift a small amount with the laying-on trowel. Use firm pressure to apply the plaster, using upward strokes as much as possible.

When the finishing coat is level with the existing plaster at the edges, draw the straightedge over it until it is flush, filling in any hollows. As the plaster begins to set, dampen it with the distemper brush to keep it workable while you trowel it smooth. Do not use too much water as this can kill the gypsum plaster in the surface and cause crazing. Wet the laying-on trowel and, keeping it as nearly flat as possible, run it over the surface in circular movements, finishing off with light upward strokes (fig. 10). If you do not achieve a smooth, flat surface at the first attempt, try again.

Patching corners
If a patch extends around an external corner, nail a batten with a smooth, straight edge to one side of the corner so that its edge is level with the existing plaster on the other side.

Designing shelf systems

Installing shelving is perhaps the easiest way to provide a home with storage and display space. And wood, which is both attractive and easy to work with, is usually the first choice as a shelving material.

When you are planning your shelving requirements, your judgement must be based on looks, function and location. For example, there is no point in using expensive materials and elaborate supports for shelves in a workshop. Nor

can you plan for a set of shelves to carry heavy books or a TV set unless you know that the wall they are to go on is capable of taking the weight.

Types of shelving

Considering what types of shelving are available is a good way to start planning. There are three main types of shelf system, which for convenience we shall call types A, B and C. Various designs are available within each type to suit all situations. They are available in a range of materials and will fit in with practically all decorative schemes and tastes.

Type A uses softwood battens to support solid wood or manufactured board shelves. Though it is only suitable for three-sided locations—such as an alcove—it is the strongest design providing the span of the shelves is not too long.

Type B standard and bracket shelving consists of vertical, slotted standards which hold brackets for the shelves themselves. Proprietary systems which use this design come with or without the shelving, but are made to suit a variety of different loadings. So if you opt for this system, make absolutely sure that the brackets and standards ، are strong enough to match your needs (fig. A).

Though some of the proprietary shelves comes with book-ends—and if you make your own shelves you can make the ends too—this type of design can look insubstantial on an open wall unless used solely for display; in most cases it is better suited to a corner, alcove or workshop.

Left: This is a self-contained type of shelf unit which is very flexible. The unit can either be made free standing or can easily be fixed to the wall. It is the ideal design to use for temporary shelving or where no obvious location for the shelving is immediately apparent. Timber standards can be used to support the shelves if the alcove walls seem to be very uneven. Otherwise one of the many different types of upright supports can be used

Location

The simplest way to build sturdy shelves is to make use of the existing house walls as supports, so look at any corner or alcove where space might go to waste.

Apart from this, the type and state of the walls are your most important considerations. With timber-framed walls, it is far better to fix through into the studs themselves, rather than to rely just on the covering, which can take only the lightest of loads.

Where the walls are very uneven or slope noticeably—as in some alcoves—simple batten supports may be impractical, obliging you to opt for type B or C shelving. So always bear in mind such restrictions before you decide on a particular design.

And in some cases, the location may also influence your choice of shelf material.

Function

Having decided on a shelf design and a location, the final form your shelves take depends a great deal on what they are to carry. In consulting the shelf loadings panel which classifies loads as light, medium and heavy, bear in mind the following points:

● Many of the materials listed are too strong to justify their expense when constructing shelves which will take only a light load.

● The span between supports is in some cases determined not by the load but by the length of unsupported material you can use without this sagging under its own weight.

● Laminated or veneered boards may be used for heavy loads with very short spans, but they are not recommended, nor is timber less than 16mm thick overall.

● Plywood and softwood have similar strengths but plywood is less likely to sag or warp.

● Shelves which are built to support heavy loads are best constructed using a solid batten system.

Estimating the width of shelves requires less judgement than the span. Where light and medium loads are concerned, all you have to do is measure the objects you wish to put on them. Remember, though, that it is false economy to buy materials that are wider than you really need; for instance, kitchen jars or spices may need only about 100mm, and paperback books around 150mm–175mm. Also bear in mind that narrower shelves require less elaborate supports than wider ones.

Only where heavy loads are to be carried does width become a critical factor. Here, the longer the length of the brackets or distance between supports, the more downward force is exerted on their fixings. Shelves wider than 300mm are definitely not recommended for heavy loads unless they are supported on three sides by a suitable batten or housing arrangement to provide even support.

Of course, there is no reason why all your shelves should be of the same width. Standard and bracket systems are available with different sizes of brackets, though you must arrange the shelves carefully or they will look out of place; graduate them evenly.

Shelving supports

Though your choice of shelving supports may already have been settled by the type of system, you may just as easily be faced with a bewildering list of alternatives. In this case, you need to consider carefully the relationship between the location, the weight and the look of the shelves.

Simplest of all supports—whether for an alcove, corner or free-standing unit— are fixed battens of metal or wood. The shelves themselves can be either secured or simply rested on the battens; and if you attach lips to the front of the shelves, these will strengthen them and help hide the battens from view.

Slightly more sophisticated are the

Safe shelf loadings

	LIGHT	MEDIUM	HEAVY
LOAD	load less than 0.75kg per 100mm length	load 0.75–3kg per 100mm length	load over 3kg per 100mm length
OBJECTS	spices, ornaments, paperback books	stereo equipment, larger books, foodstuffs	L.P. records, TV sets, heavy books, crockery
MATERIALS	glass: for very light objects man-made boards solid wood 12mm thick plywood from 9mm	thicker boards (possibly reinforced)* solid wood 15mm thick and above or plywood	strong or man-made boards at least 15mm thick (possibly reinforced)* softwood and hardwood 15mm thick and above
SPAN BETWEEN SUPPORTS	up to 610mm for rigid shelves up to 760mm for boards	up to 760mm for thicker wood or ply-wood—less for boards	maximum of 560mm for man-made boards 15mm thick 710mm for softwood 19mm thick and above 760mm for hardwood 19mm thick and above

*Boards can be reinforced by fixing battens to the underside.

various forms of bracket support, least attractive being the L-shaped steel supports commonly employed in garages and workshops. Where these are used for shelves mounted on a single wall, the entire arrangement can be made more sturdy by fixing battens to the wall and then securing the brackets to these. And in greenhouses and potting sheds, an alternative is to use heavy wooden brackets.

Wire clip arrangements actually hold the shelf from above and have the added virtue of acting as book-ends. And finally, the wide range of standard and clip-in bracket systems can all be used to support unenclosed shelving.

Enclosed shelf supports: Where your shelves are to be enclosed—either by an alcove, timber side sections or both— your choice of support is greater. In the case of a free-standing unit with its own uprights, the most difficult—but also the neatest— method is to cut housing slots in the uprights and slide the shelves into these. More sophisticated still is to use stopped housing joints so that no joins are visible at the front of the unit.

Simpler by far—but nevertheless easy to get wrong—is to screw the shelves to the uprights. Here, you are faced with the problem of screwing into end grain, which is not advisable unless you take additional precautions, such as a filler plug.

With hardwood shelves, drill pilot

A. Right: This type of shelving consists of brackets to hold the shelves, usually supported by an upright. Shelf supports are also detailed.

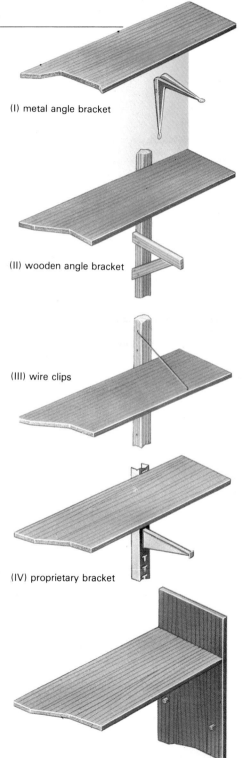

(I) metal angle bracket

(II) wooden angle bracket

(III) wire clips

(IV) proprietary bracket

(V) plug-in shelf supports

holes in the end grain slightly smaller than the threaded portion of the screws and dip the latter in PVA woodworking adhesive before you fix them. In the case of softwood or manufactured board, plug the pilot holes in the end grain with fibre plugs dipped in PVA adhesive. Make the holes themselves slightly on the generous side—both in width and depth—to avoid splitting the wood when the plugs expand.

In both cases, using double-threaded 'Twinfast' screws will make for a much more secure fixing.

Among the many ready-made enclosed shelf supports, the simplest consist of plastic or metal studs (fig. A(v)). These can be screwed directly to solid timber and plywood, or into ready-made hole liners where a soft material such as chipboard is being used. Because the shelves simply rest on the supports, they are best suited to lighter loadings.

Similar, but more substantial, are the many varieties of knock-down fitting more usually employed to joint box frame constructions.

Many self-assembly furniture kits make use of the disguised wire clip as a shelf support. For this, you need timber uprights with holes for the clips and grooved shelf ends—making softwood or hardwood the most obvious choices of shelf material.

Of the more sophisticated proprietary enclosed supports, one of the best uses two metal side brackets attached to the upright-mounted, clip-in brackets on which the shelves rest. This is both strong and attractive providing you cut small pieces out of the shelves themselves so that they fit snugly around the square U-shaped uprights. A similar system has the main support housed flush, vertically into the uprights.

Where you simply wish to use the side

B. Right: KD fittings and screwed joints can be used on free-standing units. Shelves can be hung from a metal frame or knotted cord. Bare shelves may be lipped if necessary

walls of an alcove as uprights, fittings are available which screw to the undersides of the shelves and are then jacked outwards against the walls. The pressure of the fittings against the walls holds the shelves in place and is secure enough to support medium loads safely. Because they are not permanent, the shelves can be adjusted at any time and they do not have to be cut exactly to fit.

Hanging shelf supports: Though you can buy ready-made, metal-framed hanging

(I) knock-down fittings as supports

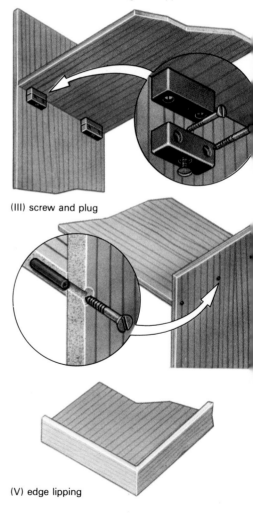

(III) screw and plug

(V) edge lipping

shelf supports, a knotted cord arrangement can often work just as well (fig. B(v)). Use a pre-stretched or non-stretch synthetic fibre cord available from yacht chandlers and figure-of-eight knots—fiddly to adjust but non-slip once they are in position.

Fixing shelves to walls

Often, the greatest difficulty with wall-mounted shelves is that the walls themselves are rarely true or evenly surfaced. This makes it absolutely essential to fix upright standards, battens or other supports in conjunction with a plumbline or spirit level. If you work carefully, even the most uneven wall can be tackled successfully.

In the case of standards, temporarily pin the first one in approximately the right position then hold a plumbline next to it to show the true vertical and mark the other fixing holes in pencil. Use the same procedure on the other standards, having first run a straightedge and spirit level between them to check the horizontal. Then drill and fix the battens into place using wallplugs and screws.

Fix vertical battens and timber uprights in the same way, having first pre-drilled their fixing holes.

When you are considering how many standards—or how much battening—to use, never be tempted to economize. Standards, though sold singly, are normally used in pairs, but fit more if the shelves are to receive heavy loads. In the alcoves, remember that a back batten in addition to two side battens will lend extra strength to the shelves themselves as well as giving more support.

As you fix uprights in place, check again with the spirit level or straightedge to ensure that these are vertical and not distorted by the surface of the wall. If necessary, use fillets of timber, cardboard or hardboard to pack out depressions or make good the unevenness.

Fixing shelves in alcoves

One of the most space-effective spots to fix shelves is in an alcove—one either side of a chimney breast, for example. This is a space that usually goes to waste but can serve as an ideal place for storage and for showing off ornaments.

When you come to cut the shelves for an alcove, measure and mark out each one individually. Though gaps between the shelves and the back wall are unlikely to show once the former are filled, unsightly gaps at the sides can be avoided by measuring for length at both the front and back of the alcove.

(II) ladder supports

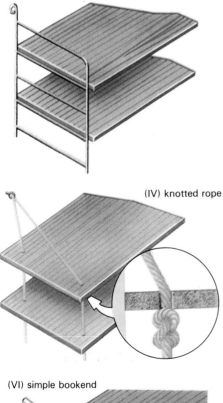

(IV) knotted rope

(VI) simple bookend

Simple ornament shelves

Storing and displaying a collection of small ornaments and mementoes can be a real problem. Small objects often look lost on standard-size shelves, and the shelves themselves take up more space than is necessary for showing small items.

This simple shelf unit solves these problems by creating what is really almost a flat pictorial display within a frame.

You can make it really cheaply from softwood battening, stained or painted to your taste. Or, for a richer look, use hardwood such as utile which is readily obtained in the sizes needed.

Make up the main frame from 25mm square stock, using glued and screwed joints. Chipboard screws give a better fixing into end grain. The only joint needed here is the central dross halving joint, which is easy to cut if you use a tenon saw and chisel.

Divide the frame into whatever divisions to suit your collection. The dividing frames again use cross halving joints and have butt joints at their ends which are secured tightly with the use of pins and glue.

When the frame is complete, sand the entire surface smooth, and finish it as you prefer. Fit suitable brackets to the top frame and screw these to the wall to support the frame.

Boxing-in

In ideal circumstances, all pipework in the house should be run out of sight—beneath the floorboards or else hidden behind walls or fitted furniture. But often, when a new central heating system has been fitted, or when new water pipes have been added, these and perhaps gas pipes as well are left exposed. This is especially likely where there are solid floors, or where vertical runs cannot be hidden inside fitted furniture such as cupboards and wardrobes.

Preliminary considerations

If you do have some exposed pipework to deal with, it is unlikely that you will be able to re-route it without going to considerable trouble and expense. The ideal solution would be to incorporate it in fitted furniture of some kind—perhaps by building a fitted wardrobe or cupboard around it. In some cases, however, sheer lack of space will make this impossible and boxing-in is the only solution.

In most cases—especially if the pipes run in a straight line, close to the wall—boxing-in is a cheap and simple operation. But even if the pipework is rather more awkward, a simple panelled timber framework will usually do the job quite adequately. All that you have to do is tailor the boxwork to your particular circumstances, though this means giving a great deal of preliminary thought to the design of the boxwork, and to the materials and finishes that you select.

Planning the work

You are unlikely to run into any insurmountable technical problems with boxing-in; the actual work involved is fairly simple. But it is the amount of time that you spend planning the work that will make the difference between an ordinary job and a significant improvement to your home.

Start by assessing the scale of the work.

If you are dealing with a single pipe, then a simple solid boxwork construction will suffice—but you must still consider whether or not you have to provide access to valves or stop taps.

One possible solution if you are covering a low, horizontal pipe is to cover the boxwork with the same material as the flooring—either by extending the carpet, or by covering it with tiles.

Further planning is necessary if you have to build a larger structure—one that covers more than one pipe, or which conceals a meter or other plumbing units. For anything other than fairly small-bore pipes running close to a wall, a framed structure will be necessary.

A typical example would be an older bathroom in which the walls are festooned with pipes that you would like to conceal. Instead of boxing-in just the pipes, it might be possible to make a bigger boxing unit that would also provide cupboard space beneath an inset basin.

Solid boxwork

In many cases, where you have a single run of pipework, this will be the most convenient technique of boxing-in. The material that you choose for the construction should be solid enough to be jointed—examples are 12mm solid timber, plywood and chipboard. A simple butt joint is usually sufficient, with the top piece resting on the side piece for strength.

As an example of the technique, if you wish to box-in a low, horizontal pipe running along a wall, start by carefully measuring the total length of the boxwork required. The height of the boxwork will obviously depend upon the height of the pipe, and the width upon the diameter of the pipe combined with the distance from the wall along which it runs. But take care if you are dealing with hot-water pipes; in this case you should allow more room and insulate the pipes first—to avoid wasting heat, and to prevent the boxwork from shrinking and splitting, particularly if you are using solid timber.

Secure the boxwork with screws to a length of 12mm square batten that is itself screwed to the wall; in most cases, this will be sufficient support, but if you wish to make the fitting more secure, you can screw a similar batten to the floor as well—making sure that you do not drill or screw into pipes or wires running beneath the floorboards.

Drill screw holes in the boxing and battens, and countersink the holes so that the screw heads will sit flush with the surface. Finish by assembling the boxing, remembering to fit the top piece above the side piece so that the finished unit has sufficient structural strength.

Three-sided enclosures: To box-in exposed pipes, start by fitting battens to the

Below: The simplest form of boxwork is solid boxwork concealing a pipe run in a corner. The materials and techniques used are very straightforward

wall on each side of the pipe and then screw projecting timbers to each of them; the timbers should project from the wall a few millimetres more than the pipe (although more space should be left for hot pipes—see above). Fit a third panel between the two timbers to conceal the pipe, securing it as detailed above.

Framework boxing

You should use this method when covering meter units, sinks and pipes that run more than a few millimetres away from the wall, and also when extra strength is required—either when the boxwork is to double as a shelf, or when it is possible that children will climb up on to the structure.

In most cases you should make the frame from 25mm square softwood, but if any heavy weights have to be supported on the finished structure, use sturdier timber such as 50mm × 25mm softwood. The members at the back of the frame are screwed directly to the wall, so there is no need to screw separate battens to the wall first.

Building the frame

The actual building of the frame is not difficult—the corners are butt-joined and secured with screws, oval nails or corrugated fasteners—so no great carpentry skills are required. However, as mentioned above, you have to take care to ensure that the positioning of the rails and side members is such that you have adequate access to the plumbing.

First, measure the overall dimensions of the area to be covered, and then make an accurate plan and cutting list.

You can build the framework over tiles or linoleum, but carpets will probably have to be cut back. When marking up the position, make quite certain that you have allowed adequate clearance all round the pipework to be covered, particularly if any hot pipes are involved.

Start the construction by fixing the back batten to the wall. You may have to make this in sections, fitted between obstructions, but in either case you

1 When boxing-in, measure up and compile a cutting list. Then fit the back batten first. Use a spirit level to make sure it is straight

2 When you have to build a frame in a corner, fit the upper end support next— then you should add the two end supports and the bottom batten

3 Make sure you check the depth of the unit by offering up the toe board and then carefully marking the position of the floor noggin on the floor

4 Firmly nail or screw down the floor noggin using the toe board as a guide. Solid floors must first be drilled and plugged to take woodscrews

should use a spirit level to ensure that the battening is level and correctly aligned.

Next make up the front frame. This consists of a member running parallel with the back batten, joined by a series of uprights. If the floor is uneven, you may need to scribe the bottom batten to fit, so do this first. Then cut the top batten to fit

and try it in position level with the bottom and the back battens. Wedge or pin the top batten temporarily in place and then check the clearance between it and the bottom batten; if the floor is uneven, the clearance may vary.

To complete the front frame, you will need vertical supports; the spacing between these will depend on the cladding material and the weight to be supported, but around 600mm is a good average. Make sure that none of the intended positions will make access to stop valves difficult, and remember that any panelling joints must coincide with the positions of the battening. Mark the support positions on the battens and check the clearance at these points to ascertain the length needed for each support batten.

Remove the battens and cut the supports to length. Make up the complete front frame using butt joints held with PVA woodworking adhesive and dowels, screws, nails or corrugated fasteners. When complete, fix the front frame in place and mark in the positions for the top supports. As with the vertical supports, their position will be governed by the weight to be supported and the access that will be required. Check the lengths of the supports needed and cut them to size. You can join them to the front frame using any of the methods described above, and at the back using dowels, corrugated fasteners or skew nails. Alternatively, you can remove the back batten entirely and nail or screw the supports from behind. Fix the completed frame to the walls.

If you want to panel your bath, build a framework as described above and fit it beneath the rim; the framework should be screwed to the floor and walls and then panelled as described below. In this case, however, you must provide access to the waste trap, either by means of a removable panel, or by designing the panelling so that it may be lifted off as a whole.

Similarly, you can box-in a sink, WC cistern or other units to include cupboards and shelves so that they become useful pieces of fitted furniture in their own right.

Fitting the panelling

Thin plywood and hardboard both make ideal panelling materials, but although hardboard is a very cheap material, it may be more difficult to finish satisfactorily. To avoid any problems with warping, you should condition the wood in the same room in which it is to be used.

Plywood is stronger and has the advantage that it can be sanded and lacquered to give an attractive, natural finish. 4mm plywood will be adequate for most purposes, but where heavy weights are to be supported, use a thicker material or add extra framing. In bathrooms, use resin-bonded marine ply.

Cut the panels slightly oversize and plane or sand the protruding edges once they have been fitted to the frame. Where panelling has to fit against a wall, this will not be possible, and you must scribe the board to fit accurately.

Fix the panelling to the framework with hardboard pins or small panel pins, set at close intervals. Before hammering make sure that the relevant section of the frame is braced against something solid. Each pin should be buried slightly with a nail punch and then covered over with a dab of wood filler which can then be sanded smooth with glasspaper.

Where you will need to remove panels in order to gain access to the pipework or stop valves, fix the panels with screws and cup washers; the latter help to spread the load of the screws on the thin panelling material as well as improving the overall appearance.

Providing access

If you are boxing-in a meter that has to be inspected regularly, then obviously a door hatch will have to be included in the boxing structure. The simplest method of making one is to cut the opening out of the front of the panelling using a jig saw. Do this before the panel is pinned to the frame, then simply fit hinges and a catch and handle.

If your completed boxwork structure is to take the form of a cupboard, do not forget that proprietary louvred or parallel doors are available in standard sizes, and these can make your boxwork look far more attractive.

5 Offer up the top front frame member and mark up any necessary joints to be made between the end supports and vertical frame members

6 Next, nail the toe board to the vertical support, then hold the support firmly in position while you nail it tightly to the floor noggin

7 Nail the top front frame member in position and offer up the top panel to check whether the corners of the room are completely square and true

8 Fix the top panel to the front and rear upper battens by screwing them from underneath, then fit the side panels to the vertical supports

Finishing boxwork

The main consideration when finishing boxwork is how to lessen the visual impact of what is essentially an intrusion on a smooth wall.

You can simply paint the boxwork, perhaps in the same color as the surroundings; if it is a fairly small construction, this will not draw too much attention to it. You may, however, have difficulty obtaining a really good paint finish on materials such as chipboard. If necessary, sand and fill the panel with a one-part fine filler paste. Alternatively, on a wallpapered wall it may be possible to hide the boxwork with matching paper.

Making window frames

Mass-produced joinery units have revolutionized the window frame business. Almost every new house built today makes use of off-the-shelf windows.

But nowadays, as the woodwork of the properties of a generation or more ago begins to fall into disrepair, the carpenter is back in demand.

To begin with it is most important to produce a rough working drawing. You will also need a list of the materials required, but this necessarily follows from the drawings.

Making a sash window

A double-hung sash window consists of a pair of pulley stiles, a head and a sill. The boxes at each side, inside which the sash weights are suspended, are formed with linings.

Making up the frame

The methods of making the joints in a sash window frame vary. The stiles are usually housed into the head and sill, while both stiles and head may be tongued to mate with grooves in the linings. The sill and head are cut wider than the frame, the protruding parts being called *horns*. The upper pair are cut off when the assembly is complete, but those on the sill are set into the brickwork at each side of the window opening when the frame is installed. The sashes themselves are of wedged mortise and tenon construction—the stiles mortised and the rails tenoned into them.

Left: A well-made sliding sash window provides excellent noise and heat insulation and, if looked after, should last for several lifetimes

First cut the head and sill to the required length—approximately 150mm wider than the actual window opening. Set them side by side on the workbench, and mark them up together with the positions of the housings for the stiles.

Next, cut the two pulley stiles to length. These must be the overall height of the frame, less the thickness of the head and sill, plus the depths of the housings into which they fit. Lay the two stiles side by side, and mark with dotted lines the areas that will fit into the housings. Then mark the four pulley positions on the stiles, and also the outline of the pocket pieces.

The slots for the pulleys are usually positioned 75mm to 100mm down from the tops of the stiles; use the actual pulleys that you will be fitting to mark out the slots.

Carefully cut out the slots with a mallet and chisel, after first drilling out the bulk of the waste wood. You can then screw the pulleys into place.

The pocket pieces can be positioned at one edge of the stile, as shown in fig. 8, or cut out from the centre.

To cut them, first drill a hole through the centre groove of the stile at one end of the pocket piece position, thread in a coping saw blade, and use the saw to cut down the groove to the other end of the piece. Now use a fine-toothed tenon saw to make the three subsequent cuts, and then chisel away the pocket piece.

Next you must cut the housings in the head and sill. Cut the housing in the head right across the width, but stop the cut in the sill.

Assembling the frame: Place the sill face up on the workbench, then glue, wedge and skew nail the stiles into place. Next glue and nail the head on to the top of the stiles, driving the nails down through the head into the ends of the stiles. Afterwards lay the frame flat on the bench, check for squareness by measuring the diagonals, then cramp it up while the adhesive sets.

Making the sashes: Making up the sashes is a little more complicated. Remember that the mortises are cut in the vertical members and the tenons on the horizontal ones. Cut the various stiles and vertical glazing bars in pairs and lay them alongside one another ready for marking out. Similarly cut the top, bottom and meeting rails, plus the appropriate number of cross glazing bars and line them all up as shown.

Now the various mortise and tenon joints can be made. Glazing bars can be joined together either with mortise and tenon joints or halving joints.

Cut the long dimensions of all the mortises slightly wider than those of their corresponding tenons so that wedges can then be driven into each joint during assembly.

The actual assembly of the sash proceeds as follows. First you must assemble the centre section of the cross bar and two vertical bars. Then cramp the bottom (or top) rail in a bench vice and drop the tenons on the H-shaped bar assembly into the mortises in the rail and place the meeting rail in position. Next, fit the outer sections of the cross bar into the mortises in the centre of the stiles, and join this assembly to the main assembly in the vice.

It is advisable to perform this operation 'dry', when you are satisfied with the fit and size of the assembly, lay it flat on the bench, cramp it up and test it for squareness. Then smother small hardwood wedges with adhesive and tap them into the overwide mortises.

Meanwhile, lay the frame flat on the bench with the outside face uppermost, so that the outside linings can be pinned in place to the edge of the head and the stiles. These are wider than the inside linings and provide a 'bead' against which the top sash bears. Next, add squaring strips to hold the frame square during installation. Then turn the frame over and pin the inside linings into place. Finally, add plywood strips to each side to enclose the weight compartments.

Installing the frame: With the sashes and frames completed, you can now install the new frame in the opening. Start by removing the old frame.

1 Make an accurate, full-sized drawing of the frame and sashes, with clear details of each joint, using the actual proprietary mouldings as guides

2 Use a sliding bevel to mark out the sloping side of the wedged mortise after you have clearly marked out the width of the mortise

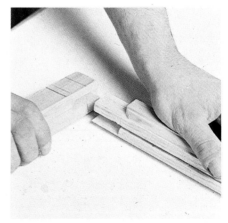

5 The top rail is joined to the vertical glazing bar with a mortise and tenon joint. Also join the cross glazing bars with a mortise and tenon joint

6 The bottom sash stiles are joined to the bottom rail with a haunched mortise and tenon; the sashes' meeting rails are jointed to the stiles

The construction of a sash frame means that any fixings to masonry walls are usually made through the head and sill of the frame; if made through the pulley stiles they would interfere with the movement of the weights and would also tend to pull the frame out of square. Try to duplicate the type, size and number of fixings found on the old window. In the case of newer windows the fixings will be ordinary galvanized woodscrews.

Drill holes for the fixings in the frame while it is still on the bench, then counterbore each hole to a depth of about

3 Having cut the pulley stiles to size, place the cord pulleys in their correct positions and firmly scribe round them prior to cutting

4 Insert the pulley stiles into the wedged housing and hammer wedges into each housing. Then place head over the pulley stiles and nail securely

7 Assemble the construction to make sure it fits and glue and cramp the completed sashes. Pin a batten across the corners. Glue and insert the wedges

8 Pin the pocket pieces, your only access to the weights and cords, in place and then screw the pulleys into the pulley stiles using the brass screws

10mm so that the screw heads will be hidden later. Afterwards offer the frame up to the opening, and use rough timber wedges to hold it in place while you mark through the fixing holes to the masonry behind with a long nail.

Now remove the frame, switch to a masonry bit, and drill holes at the marked points on the wall to take the wall plugs or expansion anchors. Having inserted the plugs, mark their positions with chalked lines then reposition the frame.

Make one final check for squareness,

9 Install the parting slip in the weight box with its tip through the head and secure it firmly in place with a small wooden wedge

10 Hold the top sash in the frame and put some parting bead into its rebate to mark where it meets the meeting rail. Then trim the meeting rail

wedging the frame as necessary, then screw it securely to the wall. Fill the bolt or screw heads with wooden plugs or filler, make good the outside of the opening with mortar, and pipe a bead of non-hardening mastic all round the frame to seal the small gap between it and the masonry.

With the frame installed, the sashes are ready to be fitted into place. If you are using the sash weights from the old window make sure that the lighter pair are fitted to the bottom sash and the heavier pair to the top one. Next, glaze the window.

Making a casement window
Casement windows are a great deal easier to construct than sliding sash windows. Mortises are cut in the horizontal members of the window frame—head and sill—and tenons are cut on the vertical members—jambs and mullions. For the casement sashes, however, the order is reversed; the stiles and bars are mortised, while the horizontal members—rails and cross bars —are tenoned into them.

The first stage in constructing a

casement window is the same as for a sash window. Cut the head and sill to the required lengths, and set these out side by side for marking out. Similarly, cut the jambs and set them out in the same way. As before, cut the head and sill wider than the actual window opening to create horns; those at the head can be cut off when the frame is installed.

Next, cut the various mortises and tenons. And, where mullions or a transom are involved, extra joints—for example, mortises in the jambs to take the tenoned ends of the transoms—will have to be cut. Note also that as with the glazing bars on a sash, the transom is usually cut into sections prior to assembly, while the mullion or mullions run unbroken from the head of the window to the sill.

Assembling the frame
With all the components cut and the joints prepared, assemble them in a dry run on the bench. The basic principle is the same as for the sash frames. First set the sill on the bench, glue the jambs into position, and finally add the head. In a frame with a mullion or mullions but no

11 Tie the top sash to the head and spring the parting beads into the pulley stiles' rebates. Pin sash cords to the bottom sash and put in frame rear

12 Pin the loose staff beads around the frame with 30mm ovals, mitring them to produce a neat joint. Finally, glaze and decorate the window.

transom, you must add the mullions at the same time as the jambs. Similarly, where a transom is involved, you must assemble the jambs, mullion(s) and transom flat on the bench, then offer up this complete sub-assembly to the mortises in the sill, and finish by adding the head as with the sash window.

With the frame assembly complete, lay it flat on the bench, cramp it up and check it for squareness. Secure the mortises with small hardwood wedges smeared with adhesive. Then, once this has set, trim the wedges flush with the frame.

Cut and mark up the components for the casements as before. But remember that, in this case, you must cut tenons on all the horizontal members and mortises on all the vertical ones. Where glazing bars are involved, the assembly follows exactly the same sequence as for the top and bottom sashes of a sash window. On a simple casement or top light which will hold only one pane of glass, you must assemble the four components in the same order as the casement frame. The joints are then similarly glued and wedged after the frame has been finally

fitted together and you have checked for square.

Installation: When the casement joints are set, clean them up all round and test the fit of the assembly within the frame. There should be a 3mm clearance all round.

Finally, hang the casements in place in the frame using galvanized hinges. Then add the rest of the ironmongery attached to the window. Screw all of the catches, handles, stays and locks into place and check that they are operating correctly.

The installation of the new frame is a relatively straightforward matter. As with the sash window frame, the horns are left on the sill, to be set into the brickwork at either side of the window opening. In this case, however, the frame is usually fixed within the opening by bolts or screws driven through the frame sides, rather than through the head and sill. To finish off, make good, weatherproof with non-setting mastic, add the interior window sill and glaze the window. Once the window is firmly in place make sure that it closes correctly and that the catches and handles all work perfectly.

Converting attics and lofts

With the high cost of housing nowadays, most people can no longer afford the luxury of a rambling attic filled with discarded bits and pieces that just 'might come in useful one day'. Space under the roof can generally be put to more practical uses.

Most homes with a sloping roof, unless it is of very shallow pitch, have an area which can be utilized in some way. For example, a restricted space or one in which people cannot stand up can still be converted into a well-designed storage unit. Larger areas offer more scope for perhaps a small study or TV viewing room, a bedroom, bathroom or a playroom. Very extensive attics might even be turned into guest suites or bedsitters.

If your attic is so small that its scope

for development is restricted just to storage space, you will still need to plan it carefully. First of all think about what you want to store there and the possible methods of doing so—shelves, cupboards, nets slung from the top of the roof or even a combination of these. Consider, too, how often you will need access to the stored items. For example, if you want to save money and bulk-buy things like canned foods, detergents and toilet rolls, you need to get at them fairly frequently. But if the area is simply to be a home for more seasonal items like garden furniture, skis or Christmas nicknacks, quick and easy access is not so important.

Try to use easily available space. If the roof slopes down to the floor, use that side for storing awkwardly shaped

objects and put shelves on the straight walls. Avoid putting too much weight on any one joist, however, as they are not designed to carry heavy loads individually.

It is a good idea to cover the joists with some form of solid flooring to avoid the risk of accidentally stepping off a joist and through the plaster ceiling of the room below. There is no need to go to the expense of laying a proper floor—sheets of chipboard which are laid side by side across the joists will be sufficient, and will also stop you damaging or dirtying any insulation there is between the joists.

If your attic is entered via a trap door you will need a ladder to reach it. An outdoor ladder brought inside when required will do if you use the attic only occasionally, but for regular use it is better to fit a folding loft ladder which is stored inside the trap door and can easily be pulled down.

The light switch is best sited on the floor below to avoid you having to stumble about in the dark looking for the switch or trap door. A multi-directional spotlamp or series of spots on a track will enable you to see what is stored all over the area.

Be sure to check that the whole area is watertight. Look at the roof to see if there are chinks of sky visible and replace any damaged tiles or fit waterproofing inside. Nail heavy-duty polythene sheets to the rafters, taking care to overlap them in such a way that they neither let rain through nor trap it. Or, for a more durable solution, put up foil-backed plasterboard which also acts as good insulation and can be painted inside to improve the appearance of the area. Choose light, bright coloured paint.

Opening up a room

It is often very difficult when crawling

Left: A very large roof space which has been given a very cosy atmosphere. Note how the original roof timbers have been cleverly blended into the design

about in a dark, confined attic to imagine how it could be opened up to provide a real room. To a large extent, what you can do depends on the planning and building laws which exist in your country or area. Since these regulations can affect markedly what you are ultimately allowed to end up with in the way of a loft conversion, it makes sense to

Below: Quite a unique way of making use of roof space is to convert it into a small kitchen. This is by no means as impossible as it might first seem. A lot of thought, however, should be given to the amount of light and headroom available and to installing all the necessary services, particularly electricity and running water, before you start the conversion work

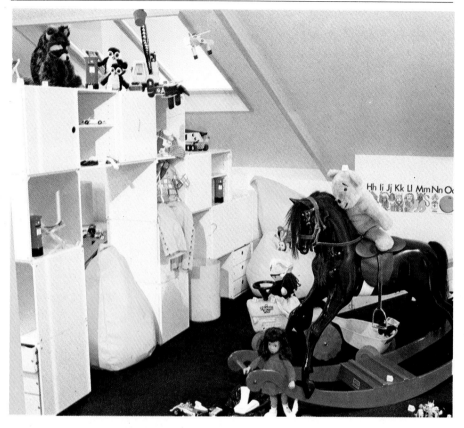

Above: Totally different, a small roof space with a simple roof light transformed into a child's playroom. Storage follows the roof slope to save space

check out your initial ideas with your local authority before getting too involved with the details.

Fire-proofing is vital since you are opening up a whole new area and some authorities may insist that not only is the new structure properly fire-proofed but that you fit self-closing hinges to every door in the house and also cover all the upstairs floors with hardboard.

While it is possible to do some alterations yourself, a major conversion generally requires professional advice and it is a good idea to consult an architect or specialist conversion firm before starting anything. They will draw up plans of the area and show you what can be done. Be clear when studying the plans about such things as usable floor area and the amount of natural light the room will get, and make adjustments as necessary. You are likely to end up with an irregularly shaped room, perhaps with one or even two sloping walls, but these are part of an attic room's charm and can be used to good decorative advantage.

While increasing the size of a house also increases its value (both rateable and saleable) it is important to make sure the extension harmonizes with the rest of the house. Try to choose window frames which match those you have already; and if you are building up the wall, use bricks or wall cladding which match those in the rest of the structure. Inside your home, complete harmony is not so essential. After all, if you are opening up a whole new floor it means you can adopt for it a whole new style.

If the attic is already reached by stairs there will be no problem with access. But if you have previously used a ladder and trap door you will need to install a staircase. And here you will need to check with your local authority for any regulations regarding type and size of staircase.

In an older house it may be possible to fit an original or specially made spiral staircase which does not look out of

place and has the advantage of blocking out very little light. But even this will take up more space then you imagine and you must make sure there is a fair-sized landing to site it on. Otherwise you can opt for a conventional closed-tread set of stairs and look for banisters to match in a secondhand or reproduction furniture retailers.

Windows are important in an attic conversion and can turn a previously dark hole into a habitable room. On the front of the house, try to match the size and scale of existing windows. But at the back—providing they are not totally alien to the design of the other windows—you might consider installing large panes to let in as much light as possible and also maximize the extent of any view you have gained.

If money is not a main consideration

Below: A teenager's room converted from an average-sized roof space. The effectiveness of the finished room belies its simplicity and low cost

and if space allows, a most attractive conversion can be made by fitting an inverted dormer window which is set back into the roof—instead of sticking out—with a small area outside. While this diminishes the space available inside the room, it does provide a small balcony for sunbathing in the summer or just giving a more attractive view. An inverted dormer would be especially good for a bedsitter or a teenager's room, especially if it overlooks the garden or some other attractive view. But if you do intend to install an inverted dormer, make sure that it is surrounded by a well-constructed wall or fence, particularly if young children are going to use the room. The balcony of an inverted dormer also makes an ideal spot for showing off plants and flowers.

Colour and design

Before choosing the decorative scheme for your new area, see how the light falls in the room at different times of day, and see how it can best be used in terms of shape. This gives you a better idea of how much light or shade is needed, how much pattern the room can take and which features need highlighting by paint or paper.

If the room has unusual angles and slopes, avoid large patterns—as well as being difficult to match when hanging, these detract from the charm of the shape and tend to overwhelm the room. Go instead for small prints or plain colours, perhaps picking out features such as beams or small areas in natural or contrasting shades.

If you prefer to retain an authentic attic feel, you might consider installing wood panelling in the form of tongued-and-grooved boarding. Hang the boards horizontally to increase the apparent size of the room, or vertically to increase its height.

For a warm, intimate feel—in a study or bedroom for instance—choose warm, dark shades of paint or wall-covering. But for rooms used in the daytime go for light colours and minimum pattern.

Where walls are uneven in texture, use a disguising covering such as hessian, anaglypta (painted in the colour of your choice) or flock. For a lighter feel use lining paper with emulsion paint on top.

Flooring should meet the needs of the room. Thick carpeting will minimize the amount of noise transmitted to the rest of the house, but sheet vinyl or cork—which are easily cleaned—are better choices if the floor is likely to become messy.

Window dressing is often a problem in an attic. Small dormers can look cluttered with thickly gathered curtains and are best fitted with a blind. Larger dormers look good with floor-length curtains, although to let in maximum light these may need to be secured with ties during the day.

Sloping windows are common in many attics and are difficult to fit with either curtains or blinds. The simplest solution here is to fix a piece of battening or a curtain pole across the bottom of the window, mounted on small blocks so that you can hang the curtains behind it. Choose a pole to match the one the curtains are hung from for an unusual and attractive effect. Bear in mind that you will need to allow extra length on the curtains for there to be enough weight for them to stay in this position.

A blind will stay in the drawn position if it is fixed firmly to a hook at the bottom of the window; on wider windows, however, you may need a hook and cord on each side.

A more expensive solution is to have a roller blind fitted between double-glazed panels though this must be more or less a permanent choice in terms of colour and pattern and is only supplied by a few specialists.

If the room is to be used mainly in the evenings—perhaps as a study, library or TV viewing room—you do not need to ensure that it is brilliantly lit. Go rather for subtle lighting effects with directional lighting placed where you need it. Spotlamps can look too harsh in this situation so choose low-level lighting in the form of lamps or wall lights.

Installing a dormer window

Above: A carefully planned dormer should look attractive from outside as well as providing enough light for your converted loft or attic

A loft conversion is a convenient way of adding space on to a house, but in most cases it is necessary to install one or more dormer windows in order to gain sufficient headroom and window light in the roof space.

Installing a dormer is, however, a large-scale undertaking, and you should not begin any work until you are sure that the finished job will be a sturdy and attractive addition to your house.

Building regulations

In all cases, you will have to apply for approval under the building regulations (local building code) for your dormer window—and, of course, for any associated work for the loft conversion itself.

You will certainly have to draw up detailed plans for submission to the building inspector. A qualified surveyor or architect can do this for you—and will, of course, know all the ins and outs of the regulations as they may affect you. But, as long as you can check through the regulations yourself, there is no reason why you should not do this work yourself.

The building inspector will be concerned to make sure that the structure you propose for the dormer window is itself structurally sound and weathertight, and that it does not make the roof any less structurally stable. You may find there is a requirement to make .

sure that it is suitably fire resistant.

If the dormer has opening windows or ventilators, these must not be situated too close to either a chimney (unless it now cannot be used) or the top of a soil or vent pipe. In the UK, the top of a chimney must be at least 1m vertically and 2.3m horizontally from the window. The top of a soil pipe should be at least 0.9m above the window if it is less than 3m horizontally from it.

Most regulations require habitable rooms to have adequate ventilation—either natural or mechanical. In the UK, the minimum area of openable window for ventilation should be five per cent of the room's floor area.

In England and Wales (except for Inner London) rooms are not strictly required to have windows (though if they do, there are complicated regulations to ensure that the space in front of them is not obstructed). But most other regulations require windows with a total glass area of between five and ten per cent of the room area.

Planning permission

In Scotland, loft conversions always require planning permission. In the rest of the UK, the loft conversion itself is not likely to require planning permission unless your house is 'listed'. Any dormer window, though, will require planning permission:

● If the dormers, together with any other extensions to the house, increase the size of the original house by more than 70 cubic metres or fifteen per cent of the size of the original house. The limit is 50 cubic metres or ten per cent for terraced houses (including end-terrace), and all house in Conservation Areas, National Parks or Areas of Outstanding Natural Beauty.

● If the dormer is higher than the ridge of the existing roof.

● If the dormer projects beyond the front of the house.

Dormer types

Before you draw up detailed building plans, you must decide which of the two main dormer types you want to install. Your decision will depend not only on the amount of extra space you want to create but on how you want the window to look once the work is completed.

Bay dormers: These are, in effect, room extensions which project to an outside wall of the house (fig. A). The bay adds maximum possible amount of space to the original loft without the need for total rebuilding and guarantees that the whole structure can be easily and safely supported on the wall below. They can be regarded by some planning authorities as constituting a fire risk and must be carefully sited to avoid this; you should check with your building inspector on the exact fire regulations which apply in your local area or county.

Roof dormers: These are lightweight structures situated partway up the roof slope (fig. B). They are sometimes built in rows, often stretching along nearly the whole length of the roof.

Roof dormers can enhance the appearance of a house if planned correctly.

However, roof dormers also have some disadvantages which should not be overlooked. Perhaps the most important is that, compared to the bay dormer, the amount of extra space they create is minimal.

A third type—the inverted dormer—is not really a dormer at all but a construction in which an area is cut away from the roof instead of being added to it. Inverted dormers are rarely used, since they add no extra space to the loft but they can be useful where an existing chimney or some other permanent structure cannot easily be removed.

If you need to create a large amount of extra space and light, think about installing a 'through' dormer—two dormers in line with one another, one on each side of the house. This also has the advantage of providing a box-shaped loft room rather than one with sloping walls.

Dormers can have flat or pitched roofs depending on the design.

Preparatory work

Once your plans have been approved by the local building inspector you can start work.

Most of the equipment you need for the work—including scaffolding and ladders—can usually be hired locally. You should also buy or hire a large tarpaulin or a number of rolls of strong polythene sheeting which can be used to cover the open roof at night in case of rain.

Dormer construction

Described in outline, dormer construction is not particularly difficult or complicated.

Figure C shows a typical dormer construction giving details of the types and sizes of materials used. The front of the dormer consists of a light 100mm × 50mm timber frame enclosing the windows.

Jointed to the front of this frame are two beams which run across the whole width of the roof. They are fixed to each set of rafters with 260mm × 12mm coach bolts. Additional support is provided by two lengths of 100mm × 100mm timber positioned where the beam crosses the existing roof. To give added stability, each support rests on a 300mm length of

100mm × 50mm timber placed on top of an existing floor joist.

A large roof beam is fitted where the dormer meets the main house roof; calculate its dimensions carefully. Add 10mm to the width of the beam and 25mm to its depth for every 300mm of the span. A beam spanning 2.4m, for instance, will need to be 200mm deep × 80mm wide. In many cases these dimensions can be made up by nailing two pieces of timber together to make a single, larger beam.

The dimensions of the lintel which stretches across the front of the frame above the window should be calculated in a similar fashion. For each 300mm of the span you should add 10mm to the thickness and 25mm to the depth of the lintel. If the span is 2.3m or more make the lintel at least 150mm thick.

The carcase is completed down both sides and across the top with lengths of 100mm × 50mm timber. These can be connected to the rest of the roofing timbers with joist hangers.

If you want to build a dormer with a small pitched roof construct it as shown in fig. C. The rafters spaced at 400mm intervals are made from lengths of 100mm × 50mm timber, with a ridge

A. Above: The Bay dormer is the most common type of window. It allows the maximum amount of space to be used within the roof or loft area

B. Above: Roof (Standard) dormers are lightweight structures sited partway up a roof slope. They look neat but add less extra space than many other types

board measuring 175mm × 13mm. The roof can be covered in felt, although tiles or slates may be more decorative.

Opening the roof

Before you cut away any of the roofing material, erect temporary supports to take the weight of the roof during construction, otherwise there would be a very real danger of collapse. For this you need two adjustable steel props and two 150mm × 50mm planks of wood slightly longer than the dormer width. Erect these as shown in fig. 1 under either the collar ties or a suitable purlin. Try to position the props to either side of the proposed dormer so they are well clear of the main building work.

With the props in position you can begin to open up the roof. You may find it easier to do this from outside but you can, if you wish, clear the entire opening from inside the roof space. Try to remove a few more tiles or slates than is absolutely necessary to give you enough space to erect the frame.

Once all the rafters are exposed, cut through each one in turn and remove it from the area.

Building the frame

Start by inserting the large roof beam positioned across the bottom of the cut-away rafters where the dormer meets the main roof. Make a neat birdsmouth joint between the cut rafter ends and the trimmer and then, to ensure that the trimmer is firmly seated, make a mitred halving joint in each end and nail it to the two adjoining rafters.

Next erect the front frame. This consists of two vertical struts making up the side frames of the window and two cross members—one resting on the wall and the second forming the window sill. In particularly wide dormers, the two cross members can be strengthened by a number of vertical struts running between them (fig. C). The struts can be skew-nailed to the rest of the frame.

The front frame should be secured by simple halving joints or by skew-nailing

one piece of timber to another; this will provide a robust structure which will not be seen once the window is complete.

Then fix the two roof beams in place. Use a mortise and tenon joint to secure the front of each beam to the top of the front frame (fig. C). You can then support the rest of the beam with a stout prop and attach it to the rafters with two 260mm × 12mm coach bolts (fig. C).

Next fit the lintel across the front of the frame. It can either be screwed to the top of the vertical uprights or securely fixed with a mortise and tenon joint. The rest of the frame can then be completed by filling the gaps along each side and across the roof with 100mm × 50mm studs spaced at roughly 300mm intervals. These are usually skew-nailed into place, although the ends of the roofing timbers often rest on joint hangers. If your design includes a pitched roof, this should now be added.

Small roof dormers are constructed along the same principles.

Cladding the outside

The exterior cheeks and gable end of the dormer can be covered in either tongued-and-grooved boarding or clad in the existing roofing material (or a mixture of both). Which you use depends on taste and the requirements of the local building regulations, but a slate or tile covered dormer often looks a lot neater and can help the dormer to blend in with the remainder of the roof.

Use 19mm chipboard to form a base for the cladding; nail it in position and then add a covering of roofing felt or waterproof paper to protect the timber. The slates or tiles themselves are hung on lengths of 19mm square battening running in closely spaced horizontal lines across the cheeks and gable end of the dormer. The exact spacings you require will obviously vary according to the size of tiles or slates you are using, but as a rough guide try to position them a half-tile or slate length apart; in this way you will achieve a good watertight overlap. Make sure the battens are well

Bay dormer construction

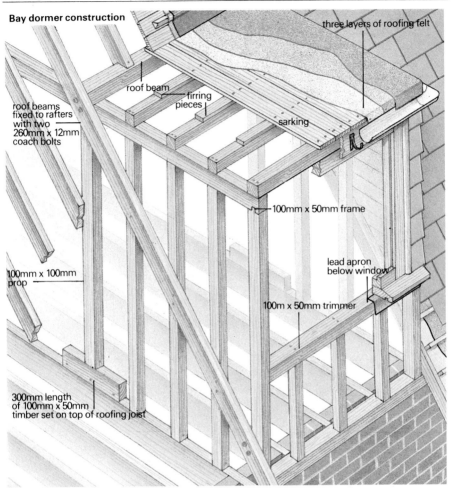

three layers of roofing felt

roof beam

firring pieces

roof beams fixed to rafters with two 260mm x 12mm coach bolts

sarking

100mm x 50mm frame

lead apron below window

100mm x 100mm prop

100m x 50mm trimmer

300mm length of 100mm x 50mm timber set on top of roofing joist

coated with preservative and fix them with galvanized nails.

Before you nail the cladding in position, fill in the gaps around the outside of the dormer with fresh roofing material. Complete the tiling beneath the window first, starting at the eaves and working up to the bottom of the window. You may find that fresh tiling battens have to be fixed in position so that you can complete the job effectively.

Fit a lead, zinc, or semi-rigid bituminous asbestos apron over the bottom of the dormer. This should stretch from the base of the window

frame, run over the top of the lower horizontal trimmer, and lap the top course of tiles (fig. 8). Extend the apron to cover at least one full tile on either side of the dormer, then dress it to follow the contour of the roof covering.

Replace the missing tiles down both sides and across the top of the dormer next. The roof on each side of the window is made watertight by nailing short sections of flashing—called soakers —to the edge of the frame, and alternating these with either slates or tiles.

The cladding can then be fixed in position. Start from the bottom and work

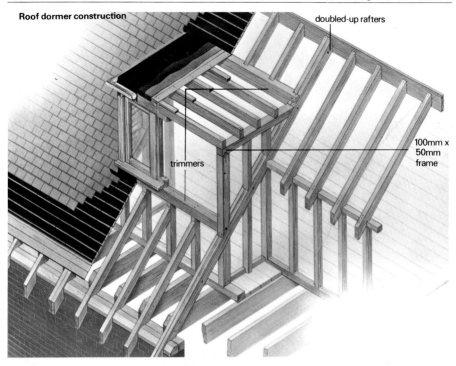

Roof dormer construction

doubled-up rafters

100mm x 50mm frame

trimmers

C. Left: Bay dormers can be built with either a flat or sloping roof.

D. Above: Doubled-up rafters and trimmers make the roof dormer very strong

upwards. The tiles or slates can be nailed either one above the other or so that their joints are staggered; use whichever method matches the existing roof. Try to ensure that each tile or slate is securely fixed and that the cladding is trimmed to fit neatly along both outside edges.

Roofing

Once the cheeks and gable end of the dormer are covered and fully water-proofed you can tackle the roof.

In the case of a flat roof, fix 19mm water-resistant chipboard laid at a slight slope on firring pieces, then 3-layer roofing felt on a layer of building paper. Ensure that the junction of the flat roof and vertical side cheek cladding is

weathered by a flashing. If you decide on a pitched roof, lay sarking felt with 150mm laps, 40mm × 25mm softwood battens treated with preservative at centres to suit the tiles. Nail the tiles to the battens and finish off at the ridge with half-round tiles bedded in mortar to match the roof tile colour.

Finishing off

All that remains is to fit a window frame and finish off the inside of the dormer. The window frame can be purchased ready-made in either wood or aluminium. It may be well worth installing double-glazing or fitting a sealed glazing unit while you are at it.

Lay a 100mm thick layer of insulation around the inside of the frame and between the rafters, then clad the interior with sheets of foil-backed plasterboard. Once the joints between the plasterboard have been covered with a thin skim of plaster, you can paint the dormer and re-decorate the roof space.

1 Before you actually begin the task of installing your new dormer window and begin to cut away any of the existing roofing material, erect two adjustable steel props—otherwise known as acrows. These are necessary supports and should be carefully placed in position under either the collar ties or a purlin

2 With your supports firmly in position, you can now begin the process of stripping the roof. Remove all the felt, battens and tiles in the designated area for the dormer. Each of the rafters, as they become exposed, should be sawn through near the top and then carefully removed

5 Now you will have to make the decision about the type of roof structure you want to use for your dormer. There are two choices—it can either have a flat or a small pitched roof. Joist hangers can be used to support the cross members if you decide on using the flat roof type of building construction used on most dormers

6 The side timbers situated along the dormer cheeks can be nailed to an adjacent rafter or continued to the floor depending on your particular style of window design. The roof of the dormer—whether flat or pitch—should then be completed using the standard methods of roofing construction, normally water-resistant chipboard covered with felt

3 Doing this sort of roofing project you really need to work very steadily and accurately. Try to open a neat hole in the roof—slightly wider than the space needed for the dormer frame—to give yourself more than enough space in which to handle all the work easily and comfortably

4 To actually build the main frame of your dormer window you will need to buy 100mm × 55mm sections of timber available from your local timber merchants. Employ simple halving joints or skew-nail one member to another to really provide a robust and safe building structure

7 A lead, zinc or bituminous flashing strip can now be fixed to the top part of the frame. You should also fit an apron to the underside section. The window frame can then be fitted in either at this stage or when the dormer has been completely finished off. You should screw or nail the window securely to the actual dormer frame

8 Now your new dormer window is almost completed. The last stage of building to finish the construction is to dress the apron—whether it be lead, zinc or bituminous—carefully over the lower tiles of the adjacent section of the roof of the house. It should be lapped for at least 100mm to ensure complete water-tightness at this important junction

Greenhouses and conservatories

A conservatory is one of the most delightful ways of adding more space to your home. You can add a space for casual dining to the exterior of the house. Access is through the living room, but, to make the serving of food convenient, the window has been turned into an open hatch giving a very pleasant view from either side.

Hanging plants and the light-coloured cane furnishings add to the bright, cheery atmosphere. In a conservatory it is best to choose light colours to keep the room from becoming dreary on rainy days. Select furniture that can easily be moved from outdoors to indoors. A slate floor (or you could use tiles instead) gives an outdoor feeling to the room and is very resistant to water. Other types of flooring may be spoiled when watering plants.

Right: A casual, airy dining area can be created by attaching a room to the back of the house. **Below:** A neat greenhouse, which can be filled with plants, can be built as a small extension to your kitchen window

The serious plant lover may find in time that the addition of a greenhouse in the back garden is the best place for putting a growing collection of house plants. You can grow tender, flowering potted plants that include pelargoniums and fuchsias give a splash of colour to the garden throughout many months of the year. In the summer you can place them outdoors or bring them inside the house for special occasions.

Perhaps the smallest practical greenhouse is one that is built as an extension to your kitchen window. An array of colourful flowering plants, especially in the winter months, gives you something pleasant to focus on when you are doing the washing up. A small kitchen greenhouse is the ideal spot for growing herbs that will not only add a decorative touch to the kitchen but will provide a convenient means for getting the right ingredients to cook good food.

Exterior walls at right-angles are an ideal area to add a conservatory to your house. A patio can be converted into a conservatory, but still retain the feeling of being outdoors.

The warmth created by sunshine, however, means that the patio can be enjoyed for a longer time of the year. It means also that outside walls in the home receive extra insulation especially when, as in the picture, there are several French windows which would otherwise be a source of draughts.

Wrought iron supports are a lovely decorative touch—they were widely used in Victorian times, which is when conservatories became common.

Left: You can easily convert your patio into a bright conservatory with some simple building work

Below: To give a different look to your garden you can construct an attractive gazebo greenhouse

Above: To prevent your plants from being scorched in the conservatory, a roller blind on the roof can be the ideal answer

Beautiful arched and stained glass windows can give a conservatory a very special quality, and it can be greatly enhanced by rows of plants that extend the width of the wall.

Your plants need not take up precious room space in the conservatory. The addition of shelving may be all that is needed for grouping your plants.

In a conservatory with glazed ceiling panels, protection is often required during periods of the day when there is strong sunlight—otherwise plants could scorch and the room would become unbearably hot. A roller blind is a very good idea as it will diffuse light coming into the room; bamboo blinds also keep out some sunlight. For a really good screening your best bet is an inexpensive blind of pinoleum—very fine wood strips woven with cotton.

Whether you are thinking of attaching a conservatory to your house or building a greenhouse in your garden, you need not limit yourself to the usual traditional designs. You could in fact construct a very charming greenhouse in the style of a Victorian gazebo. A number of prefabricated greenhouses exist, which when installed in your garden, will not only be functional but add to its overall appearance. The gazebo-type of greenhouse can also provide a pretty and tranquil place for sitting and relaxing.

But the important thing to consider when choosing a particular design of greenhouse—or conservatory for that matter—is that it fits in with its surroundings. Natural wood and a geometric shape can complement the straight lines of paving stones and flower beds. But formality can be well balanced by a more informal layout of items like the rockery and by the choice of flowering shrubs and other plants.

Below: A large greenhouse filled with flowering plants throughout the year can really add colour to your garden

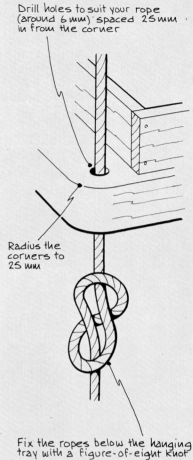

Drill holes to suit your rope (around 6 mm) spaced 25 mm in from the corner

Radius the corners to 25 mm

Fix the ropes below the hanging tray with a figure-of-eight knot

Left: The hanging rack can hold many plants on three levels to dress up windows or hide awkward corners

Hanging rack for plants

Display your plants in this simple hanging rack. You can hang it across a window where the plants will get plenty of light or fit it into a corner.

Make each tray from softwood boards. You can buy plastic flower trays to take your plant pots and stop drips. Use these to give you the size of the trays. Finish the timber with lacquer.

Fix the trays on four ropes tied to hooks on the ceiling, and tie off under the trays at equal heights.

INDEX

The numbers in **bold** indicate detailed projects and the *italic* numbers refer to pictures.